ANTONIO CARLUCCIO'S
PASTA

ANTONIO CARLUCCIO'S
PASTA

Photography by Laura Edwards

Quadrille
PUBLISHING

EDITORIAL DIRECTOR **Jane O'Shea**
CREATIVE DIRECTOR **Helen Lewis**
PROJECT EDITOR **Simon Davis**
EDITOR **Susan Fleming**
ASSISTANT EDITOR **Romilly Morgan**
PROJECT DESIGN & ART DIRECTION **Claire Peters**
DESIGN ASSISTANT **Emily Lapworth**
PHOTOGRAPHER **Laura Edwards**
PHOTOGRAPHER'S ASSISTANT **Kim Lightbody**
FOOD AND PROPS STYLIST **Anna Jones**
FOOD STYLIST'S ASSISTANT **Emily Ezekiel**
PRODUCTION **James Finan, Vincent Smith**

First published in 2014 by
Quadrille Publishing Limited
Alhambra House
27–31 Charing Cross Road
London WC2H 0LS
www.quadrille.co.uk

Text © 2014 Antonio Carluccio
Photography © 2014 Laura Edwards
Design and layout © 2014 Quadrille Publishing Limited

ISBN 978 1 84949 370 3

Printed in China

For an amazing seven decades I have been loving, making, cooking and eating pasta! I know that my pasta-consuming career must have started more than 70 years ago, because I would have eaten pasta shortly after I was born in 1937. The first solid that Italian babies enjoy, after about four months, is inevitably pasta, which in my case – and in the lives of many other Italians – marked the beginning of a lifelong passion.

No other food is more Italian and more satisfactory to eat than pasta. Pasta can be prepared at any time, anywhere in the world, in any situation, for any occasion, and can be presented as a snack or main course, a complete meal or even as a dessert. It can be made fresh – from a combination of wheat flour and water only, perhaps with the addition of egg – but, and this is the most significant thing about pasta, it can also be bought dried, when it is made from the self-same ingredients, so it is very readily available. It can also be cooked in minutes – whether, long, short, straight or convoluted – and its variety of shapes can be served with a multitude of different sauces.

Pasta is also very healthy, although it has not always enjoyed such a good reputation. In the 1960s and 1980s, pasta was accused of being responsible for the spreading waistlines of many Italians. There were cries to ditch it as a staple food until some eminent nutritionist from America brought the welcome news that pasta, eaten with consideration, is an excellent food and a valued part of the famed Mediterranean diet. Indeed, pasta is considered one of the most versatile ways of gaining energy from food: it is basically a carbohydrate, but is easy to digest. It also takes a long time to digest, so its slow-release energy is invaluable to athletes: I believe, for instance, that many marathon runners eat a large plate of pasta some time before their race, as do rugby players before an important game. With the addition of fat, meat, fish or cheese, a pasta meal provides protein, while the tomato and other vegetables in the sauces give the body necessary amino acids, calcium and precious vitamins.

Because of the increasing popularity of pasta, it has assumed the status of *piatto unico* – a complete meal – making the classic Italian meal of three to four courses, especially on a daily basis, superfluous. I don't need to say how beneficial this might be to the weight and health levels of the average Italian... I must admit, though, being the age I am, that I still like to eat a little pasta, at certain meals, in between the *antipasto* and the meat or fish course.

I have written eighteen books on Italian cooking, each of which has mentioned pasta, and one of which specialised in pasta itself. It may seem repetitious to be producing yet another, but there are so many possibilities in the culinary pasta palette, that I thought (with the encouragement of my publisher) that we could produce something that would still be of value. There are, after all, more than 600 shapes of pasta produced in Italy, with perhaps even more varieties of sauces, so there are a few ways in which to explore new territory! It is obviously impossible to ignore the very classic Italian pasta dishes, so those few are here again, albeit in a slightly different form, but they are accompanied by many which are new, created completely afresh by myself, or newly adapted from regional and national recipes which reflect the many aspects of authentic Italian cuisine.

The most important thing that I would like to give you all is a taste of the experience, love and passion I possess, which will help to make it easy for you to reproduce some of these pasta dishes for yourself. I won't be upset if, in some cases, you use more or less of my suggested ingredients. I would, however, be a little 'hurt' if you added garlic and oregano to a bolognese sauce. That is a step too far for me...

So in this book I hope I am able to distill my pasta knowledge – the recipes, tips and secrets I have collected with passion over the last fifty years, in order to allow you to recreate, in many different ways, this most popular and delicious dish in the world. Good luck and *buon appetito!*

— PART ONE —
ALL ABOUT PASTA

THE HISTORY OF PASTA

Many diverse ethnicities have contributed to the creation of what we now call pasta. The concept is not exclusively Italian, nor Chinese, Etruscan, Ancient Greek or Roman. Many think the original inspiration was Arab, but no one really knows. The subject is a complete minefield, and the origins of pasta are as tangled and slippery as a bowl of cooked spaghetti!

'Pasta' is the term applied to foods made from an unleavened dough of grain flour and water. Chinese and Japanese noodles are made from combinations of liquid and various ground grains, seeds and even a root, and they have been in existence for thousands of years. But can they be called pasta? Similarly, can the unleavened doughs which form the wrapping of dumplings in Russian and Slav – not to mention Chinese – cuisines be thought of as pasta? The flour and water mix may not have originated in Italy, but the use of the Italian word 'pasta' – or 'maccaruni' as it was often called in early texts – conjures up the image of a uniquely Italian product, which is cooked by boiling in water, then sauced.

Even if the Chinese were the first civilisation to make a version of pasta, it is not true that the Venetian traveller Marco Polo brought the idea back to Italy from China in the late 13th century. For a start, the soft noodles he encountered in China were made from sago, breadfruit or millet pastes – not the wheat paste which is now acknowledged to be the basis for pasta – and his writings reveal that he already knew of the existence in Italy of wheat-based pastas such as vermicelli and lasagne, most of them known by the generic name of 'maccaruni'.

The Etruscans, a pre-Roman civilisation in the Italian peninsula, are thought to have been one of the first to make pasta. Reliefs in the *Tomba Bella* in Cerveteri illustrate what look like a pasta board, a rolling pin and a pasta wheel. But this proves nothing, and texts at this date suggest that any alimentary paste was more likely to have been baked than boiled. The same is true of many Ancient Greek and Roman equivalents. For instance, Aristophanes mentions *laganon*, a flattened dough, in his 5th-century BC comedy *Lysistrata*; this was similar to the *laganum* or *lagane* of the Romans, and both seem to have been baked as a type of bread. ('Lasagne' is thought to derive from these words, so there could be at least a linguistic connection.) But it is often unclear whether bread, biscuits, pastry or pasta is being talked about in many of the ancient textual sources, for many simple flatbreads and biscuits – including the famous hardtack – are a basic combination of flour and water.

In the 1st century BC, the Roman poet Horace wrote in his *Sermones* about going home to have a meal of *porri et ciceris laganique catinum*, a bowl of leeks, chickpeas and *laganum*. This suggests vegetables mixed or cooked with something like pasta, and to this day in Puglia, *ciceri e tria*, a soup of chickpeas and pasta, is still served (see page 63). In this dish, some of the pasta, usually tagliatelle, is cooked in the soup, while occasionally some is also deep-fried until crisp.

This crispness might give more satisfaction in terms of texture in the mouth, and in fact I think that this idea may contribute to the origins of the modern pasta term *al dente* – an explanation for which I have been seeking all my pasta-researching and pasta-eating life! In the beginning, pasta was a food for the Roman nobles. Gradually, over the centuries, it became a food for the poor, who cooked it 'to the tooth' so that its texture could more closely emulate that of the meat they could not afford.

The word '*tria*' in the *ciceri e tria* previously mentioned comes from the Arabic for noodles, *itriyah*. Interestingly, in Morocco sheets of an unleavened dough are used to make a layered pie similar to lasagne, called *trid* (once the favourite food of the Prophet Mohammed). This to me would seem to confirm the Arabic influence on the origins of pasta in Italy. The Arabs conquered Sicily in the 10th century AD, and texts thereafter talk of a form of pasta that was dried. A 12th-century Arab geographer, Al-Idrisi, recorded that semolina in strands was common in Sicily. (Sicily had an ideal climate for the production of durum or semolina wheat, and for drying the pasta made from it.)

In many regions pasta gradually became a vital staple for feeding hungry families: it was filling, it was cheap, and could be sauced by vegetables, not just with expensive meat. In fact, very quickly it became an accepted dish for the whole of Italian society, exemplified by the number of attempts to industrialise pasta-making. No less a genius than Leonardo da Vinci tried to do this: his *Codex Atlanticus*, a collection of drawings and writings from the late 15th century, has sketches in it by the master for a lasagne-making machine (it didn't work!).

By the end of the 16th century, written distinctions were being made between maccaruni and vermicelli, and by the beginning of the 17th century a *ngegno da maccaruni* had appeared that could push hard dough through a die, making maccaruni with a hole in the centre. In the early 19th century, the Buitoni family opened the first mechanical pasta factory in Italy (and the world): many of the processes were still quite primitive, with workmen apparently kneading the dough with their feet!

One of the principal qualities contributing to pasta's longevity in culinary popularity was, of course, its ability to last well. Because fresh pasta could be dried, it had a long shelf life, and could and did spread throughout the whole of the rest of Italy and the Mediterranean basin, and all points north and south. Its durability also meant that it was able to be taken on long sea voyages, so it could be claimed that the dried pasta of Italy might have enabled the discovery of the New World.

In the United States, pasta became one of the nation's favourite foods. Thomas Jefferson did not introduce pasta to the US – a pasta myth like that of Marco Polo – but he was interested enough to ask for a mould for making maccheroni (macaroni) to be sent to him, and shipped in two cases of pasta in 1789. Pasta was soon being manufactured in the States, and new dishes invented: spaghetti and meatballs is something we did not know in Italy. The horror that is canned pasta was invented in America – possibly how many Britons were also introduced to pasta, in the form of the infamous canned spaghetti in tomato sauce. And to this day I think the Americans cook pasta for too long, until it is well beyond *al dente* (and indeed some US manufacturers do not use durum wheat semolina, which means the pasta will be fairly soft to start with). Possibly introduced originally by the British, but treated in the States almost as a national dish, macaroni cheese apparently was what most Americans cooked after the horrific events of 9/11, 2001, the ultimate comfort food.

WHAT IS PASTA?

As stated earlier, pasta basically is a mixture of a grain flour and water. There are two main groups of pasta, fresh and dried. Obviously all pasta starts off as fresh, and much of it is served thus. But the pasta which the Arabs introduced to Sicily so many centuries ago was dried after it was freshly made, and the drying of pasta has been a basic part of pasta-making (and of big business) ever since. Many people think that fresh pasta is superior to dried, but there really is no comparison. Fresh is not inherently better, it is just *different* to dried. Fresh pasta is made to be eaten 'soft' to the mouth, whereas dried pasta, if cooked correctly, gives that inimitable and quintessentially Italian *al dente* texture, which is definitely not soft.

In Italy the grain used in pasta-making is principally wheat, although buckwheat pasta is found as well. Dried pasta is typically made from a particular wheat which grows most successfully in the Italian climate, commonly known as hard wheat, semolina or durum wheat (*Triticum durum*). The wheat used today in pasta-making (grown mostly elsewhere in the world, as Italy cannot supply all her own needs) has been developed from emmer (*Triticum dicoccum*), an ancient or relict type of wheat now grown by Italian farmers as an IGP (*Indicazione Geografica Protetta*) product, this is an EU regulation that protects authentic foodstuffs of any given region. It is known in Italy as farro, and demand for it has led to yet another variety of wheat,

spelt (*Triticum spelta*) being substituted for emmer. (Spelt, emmer and einkorn flours and dried pasta are all available from good delicatessens.)

Dried pasta – *pasta secca* – by Italian statute can contain nothing but durum wheat and water. The wheat is unique because of its high levels of protein and gluten and its low moisture content, which differentiates it from soft or bread wheat (*Triticum aestivum*), which we think was the grain most familiar to the Ancient Greeks and Romans. The glutens of durum wheat prevent the pasta stretching and breaking while it is drying, and also help the pasta retain its texture and taste during the cooking process. And indeed the drying process itself can affect the taste and cookability of dried pastas. Commercial pastas are often dried quickly at very high temperatures, which can drive out flavour. Much better are the traditional, artisanal pastas, which are dried at lower temperatures over a period of perhaps days.

Durum wheat is also used, in Morocco, to make cracked wheat or bulgur as well as couscous – which, along with the Sardinian fregola, are probably very like some of the earliest known 'pastas'.

Fresh pastas are often made from wheats other than durum: the finely milled Italian *doppio zero* or '00' flour is made from a softer wheat, which has a medium gluten content, which is ideal for fresh pasta and pizza. Sometimes manufacturers mix different types of flour for different effects. Both fresh and dried pastas can be made with the addition of eggs.

TYPES OF PASTA

Italians eat about 30kg of pasta per head annually, and about eight large commercial companies, plus numerous small artisanal companies, produce 3 million tonnes of pasta every year. Most of this is dried. But there are so many different types of pasta, so many different ingredients, and such varying methods of production, that it can all be quite confusing. It might help to define all these differences more closely.

Pasta Secca di Semola
{ dried durum wheat semolina pasta }

This is the basic dried pasta, and it is made from a paste of durum wheat semolina flour and water only. Another essential difference between fresh and dried pasta is that fresh pastas are made and cut by hand. Dried pastas are extruded by machine through dies to make many different shapes. The lengths of machine-made pasta are cut to different lengths, which introduces yet another set of categories.

PASTINA OR PASTA CORTA MINUTA (VERY SHORT PASTA)
These are the tiny shapes made for use in broths and soups – *pasta per brodo* – and include stelline, ditalini and anellini.

PASTA CORTA OR PASTA TAGLIATA (SHORT PASTA)
This category contains pastas which are larger than the ones for broth, and includes many of the familiar 'shaped' pastas such as farfalle and fusilli, and also some of the hollow tubular pastas such as penne and macaroni. These short pastas are the ones that are eaten with just enough sauce to coat them – as *pasta asciutta* (see page 66) – or baked in timbales (see page 168). Some short pastas can be fresh as well as dried.

PASTA LUNGA (LONG PASTA)
These, obviously, are the long extruded dried pastas such as spaghetti, capelli d'angelo and bucatini (round in basic shape), linguine (a more flattened shape), and tagliatelle and fettuccine (which are ribbons or bands of pasta). Some long pastas can be fresh as well as dried.

Pasta Fresca di Semola
{ fresh durum wheat semolina pasta }

This, like the basic dried pasta above, is made from a mixture of fresh durum wheat semolina and water. But instead of being dried, it is served fresh. It is mainly produced and eaten in the south of Italy, most particularly in Puglia. It is more difficult to make than most fresh pastas which are made with flours other than durum wheat semolina, and it also takes longer to cook. Its texture in the mouth, because of the glutens, is also tougher than other fresh pastas. It is virtually chewy, and because of this is a perfect partner to the robust *ragù* made in this area. The most famous Pugliese shape is orecchiette (see page 19), but you can also find fusilli, cavatelli and strozzapreti. Sardinia also produces a fresh durum wheat semolina pasta in the form of malloreddus or gnocchetti sardi.

Pasta all'Uovo Secca
{ dried egg pasta }

You might think that egg pastas are principally made at home, but egg is used in many commercial pastas too. In fact the combination of egg, durum wheat semolina and water can only be used in commercial pastas, as the dough – because of the glutens the semolina contains – is far too firm to be mixed properly at home. This particular pasta dough is usually cut into ribbons of various sizes, which are coiled into nests after drying, and packaged in those same nests. This dough is also used to make commercial stuffed pastas such as tortellini or ravioli. I feel that many industrially produced dried egg pastas are fine – tagliatelle is a good larder stand-by, for instance – but I cannot say I like any stuffed pasta other than homemade.

Pasta Fresca all'Uovo
{ fresh egg pasta }

This is the pasta you would make at home and is about the only one not made with durum wheat semolina. It is usually made with Italian '00' flour, a plain or all-purpose flour from a tender wheat usually used to make cakes (and bread).

The combination of '00' flour and eggs makes for a very malleable dough that can be cut into many shapes, from long (square spaghetti, tagliatelle and lasagne), to short (farfalle, triglie and fusilli). This is also the pasta to use for the most delicious stuffed pastas such as tortelloni, ravioli and cappellacci. The Emilia-Romagna region has long been known for the quality of its egg pasta, both fresh and dried, and many of the most famous fresh stuffed pasta shapes originated here.

This fresh pasta is also the one that can be coloured: add spinach for a green dough, beetroot for a red dough or cocoa if making a sweet pasta (see page 31).

Pasta Speciale
{ special pasta }

What I call 'special' pastas are generally available commercially and dried, and encompass the pastas made for those suffering from coeliac disease and wheat intolerance, and the few pastas made with flours other than wheat. Maize or rice flours, for instance, are often used for some of the gluten-free pastas now commonly available in many of our larger supermarkets. Only a few shapes are available as yet, but more may come.

These pastas do not react in quite the same way to cooking as wheat pastas, primarily because they are pure starch, rather than a combination of starch and protein (gluten) as in wheat. Rice pasta can be sticky if it is overcooked, but its neutral flavour is fine with sauces. Corn or maize flour pastas can become tough as they cool, but the flavour is good. In general gluten-free pastas cook in less time than ordinary pastas, so keep your eye on them. (Potato and tapioca flours are also available for those who want to avoid gluten in cooking, but they are not used, to my knowledge, in commerical pasta-making.)

Chestnut and buckwheat flours are also gluten-free, and the latter is used in Italy to make the pizzoccheri noodles found in Lombardy, in the Valtellina valley: buy them in packets, as the flour is quite difficult to come by. Despite its name, buckwheat is not related to wheat, as it is not a grass: it is actually related to sorrel and rhubarb! Buckwheat flour is used in the making of Japan's soba noodles, and many pancakes: among them Russian blinis and Breton galettes.

DRIED PASTA

MAFALDE
long rectangular ribbons, with one or both sides ruffled

SPAGHETTI
long rounded strands of fresh or dried pasta, of varying thickness, in this case *integrale* (wholewheat)

TAGLIATELLE
long ribbon pasta, usually 5mm wide, generally narrower than fettuccine

ANELLINI
thin rings of dried pasta from Sicily, for *brodo*

FARFALLINE

bow tie or butterfly
shapes with a ridged
edge, for *brodo*

PENNE

medium-length tubes or
'quills' cut diagonally at
both ends

PIZZOCCHERI

buckwheat tagliatelle,
from northern Lombardy

CAPPELLI

pasta made from durum
wheat semolina flour in a
shape that reminds one
of a well-worn sun hat

PACCHERI

a tube-shaped pasta
of varying length and
diameters

FRESH PASTA

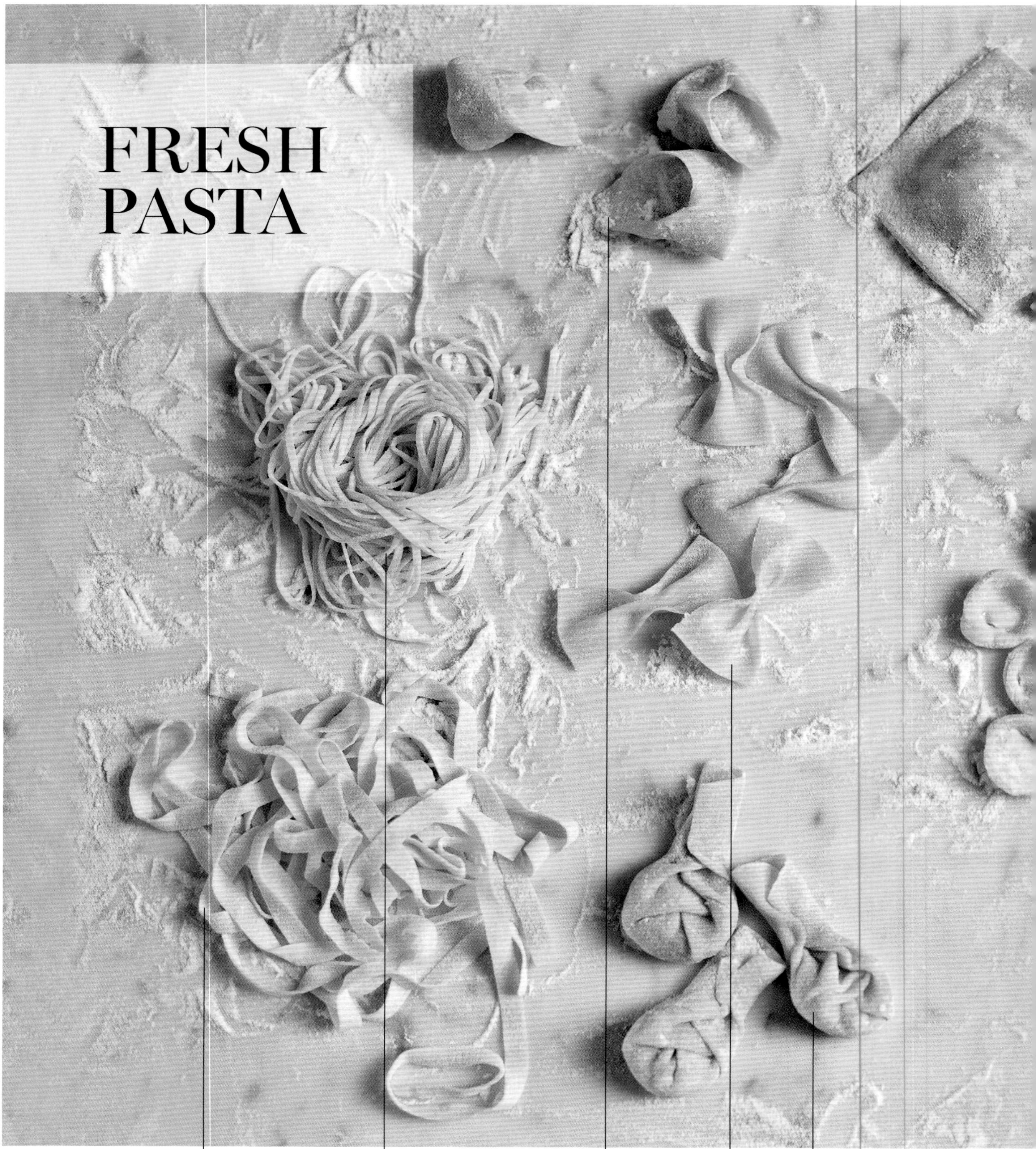

TAGLIATELLE

fresh tagliatelle is best for thick meaty sauces such as *ragù*

TAGLIOLINI

a variety of tagliatelle that is thinner and cylindrical in shape

CAPPELLETTI

meat or vegetable filled 'little hats', traditionally served *in brodo*

FARFALLE

pinched in the centre, these bow-tie or butterfly pasta are best suited to cream or tomato sauces

CULURGIONES

Sardinian plaited ravioli stuffed with a variety of different fillings

RAVIOLI
the most ubiquitous
of filled pastas, stuffed
in a manner of ways
depending on the area
where they are prepared

ORECCHIETTE
made from eggless
dough, this ear-shaped
pasta is good with
vegetable sauces

FUSILLI
a long, thick, corkscrew-
shaped pasta, its twists
and turns are good for
holding chunky sauces

MALTAGLIATI
meaning 'badly cut',
these pasta pieces are cut
from the dough with a
knife in irregular fashion

PASTA AND SAUCES

A central philosophy of Italian pasta cooking is matching the right pasta to the right sauce. Certain types of sauces are best for fresh pasta, for instance, some are better for dried: some sauces are perfect with long pastas, some with short.

In general, the smoother the pasta, the thinner the sauce; the more convoluted the pasta shape, or the rougher the outside of the pasta, the thicker the sauce. (In fact, new pasta shapes are being invented all the time, purely to create something that will hold a sauce in the most delicious way.)

Regionally, throughout Italy, there are many different types of pasta, sauces and combinations; it is not an exact science. But the more you explore the magic world of pasta, the more you experience dishes from a restaurant or home, or indeed books, the better you will be at making your own informed choices when cooking and saucing pasta.

If you make your own fresh pasta at home, the sauces that will accompany it will be the simplest – butter and lemon juice or a basic tomato sauce for capelli d'angelo, or angel's hair, for instance. Tagliolini, the smallest form of tagliatelle, is particularly good with truffle and other delicate sauces using the subtle flavours of crab or lobster. Melted butter infused with a few sage leaves is all that many a homemade stuffed pasta requires.

Dried spaghetti and other round and long dried pastas are suitable for most sauces. But please, do not use spaghetti for *bolognese*. The ideal pastas for *bolognese* are fresh egg tagliatelle, or dried egg or eggless tagliatelle. Being a flat ribbon of pasta, tagliatelle has more 'edges' than the smooth and round lengths of spaghetti, providing a different sensation for the 'sensitive' Italian palate. The combination of spaghetti and *bolognese* seems to have been an invention of the British, and I do urge you to change your ways!

Short dried pastas like macaroni (maccheroni in Italian) and penne are good for *arrabbiata* or long-cooked meat and tomato *ragù*. If the pasta is ridged (*rigate*) rather than smooth (*lisce*), the sauce will adhere more to it. The extruding dies used to produce commercial dried pasta are now usually made of metal and Teflon, which produce a smoother surface; traditionally, in Puglia, for instance, the dies are made of bronze, which leaves a certain roughness on the pasta extruded, making the sauce adhere better. If the pasta is curved, like orecchiette, for instance, the curve creates a reservoir in which nuggets of a thicker sauce can gather.

Meat Sauce or Ragù

The Italian word *ragù* comes from the French *ragoût*, meaning a well-seasoned stew of meat or fish, and vegetables (coming from the Old French *ragouster*, 'to revive the taste'). These sauces, like most Italian dishes, are generally started off with a *battuto*, or sauce base. Once a mixture of *lardo* and flavourings, 'beaten' or finely chopped to amalgamate, was used. But more often now olive oil or butter is mixed with flavourings such as onion or garlic (even both sometimes), diced carrots and celery, and herbs and spices. The *battuto* can be plain or can have added tomatoes to give more colour and taste. This is then fried to soften it, when it becomes a *soffritto*. The meat is then added, either chopped up or whole, and this can be beef, pork, veal or a mixture, lamb or game (even fish).

RAGÙ ALLA BOLOGNESE

This is the best-known *ragù*, so called because it originates in the city of Bologna, in the region of Emilia-Romagna. The locals eat this sauce exclusively with tagliatelle. *Spaghetti bolognese*, on the other hand, is a failed attempt by foreigners, especially the British, to copy the original. The failure consists of using only beef, which is often very fat and greasy, as a base, with garlic and a mixture of herbs that often include the very overwhelming oregano, basil, parsley, rosemary and sage. The ultimate insult, however, is using a dried 'Italian herb mixture'. Nothing could be worse than that, because what you want from a *bolognese* is the pure taste of the combination of beef and pork, beef and veal or veal and pork, with nothing else but onion, wine, tomato pulp and tomato paste.

RAGÙ ALLA PUGLIESE

In Puglia a very similar *ragù* to the *bolognese* is produced using lamb instead, perhaps with the addition of pieces of spicy pork sausage. The pasta used in this region, however, is different, and can include orecchiette, strascinati, lasagnette, linguine, bucatini and even gnocchi or naturally tagliatelle, all made just with durum wheat semolina and water, without eggs. The cheese used at the end could be Parmesan, provolone, caciocavallo or an aged pecorino.

RAGÙ ALLA NAPOLETANO

The Neapolitan *ragù* is something special, eaten mostly on Sundays, is something of a ritual. Here not mince is used but larger pieces of beef and specially the *scamone*, a cut from the rump, possibly with bones, and also a piece of pork, which is cut and served with the sauce to dress larger shapes of pasta, like maccheroni, spaghetti, fusilli, paccheri, ziti, candele, penne, rigatoni, etc. The beef itself is eaten as the main course, after the dressed pasta. Instead of one piece of beef, very typical is the use of little rolled escalopes of beef stuffed with a piece of lard, parsley, garlic and grated Parmesan. These are rolled similarly to beef olives and pinned with a toothpick. This is eaten as a *piatto unico*, a main dish, where one *braciola* is served with the pasta and sauce, sprinkled with Parmesan or pecorino. Many food historians believe this classic Italian dish was what inspired the uniquely American dish of pasta and meatballs.

Tomatoes and Tomato Sauces

Tomato sauce seems to be so inextricably associated with Italian pasta dishes that it may come as a bit of a surprise to learn that Italy was not aware of the tomato until the 16th century. The tomato was among the new foodstuffs the exploring Spaniards brought back from the New World, along with potatoes, sweet and chilli peppers, avocados and turkeys. The first Italian tomato was obviously paler than the red globes we know today, as it was given the name of *pomo d'oro*, or 'golden apple'.

Although introduced so many centuries before, the tomato was not commonly used, certainly not in sauces for pasta, until as late as the 19th century: it is said the Duke of Buonvicino offered a recipe for *vermicelli con lo pommodoro* in 1839. However, only a few decades later, Italian cookery books were full of recipes for tomato sauces, tomato purées, tomato pastes and soups. And it was around 1900 that a Neapolitan company – for tomatoes grew best in the warm south – started one of Italy's main exports by canning the local tomatoes. It is also said the advent of liquid sauces such as tomato meant that forks had to be used to eat pasta (until then it was eaten with the fingers). So it could be claimed, much as pasta might have contributed to the discovery of the New World, that the use of the New World tomato might have contributed to the advancement and development of European table manners!

It is these canned tomatoes that will probably be the best for using in countries other than Italy, for not many places can provide the flavourful, sun-ripened tomatoes we enjoy. The tomato industry also provides you with their products in jars, tubes and cartons.

PEELED PLUM TOMATOES

Plum tomatoes, Roma or San Marzano, are the tomatoes usually employed for canning purposes, as they have a greater solid to liquid ratio than other tomatoes. Whole peeled tomatoes are also known as *pelati*. They are available whole or chopped, usually in tomato juice, in both cans and jars. Whole tomatoes will contain most of the seeds, and all of the liquid: as a result, you will have to cook sauces made from these for longer than you might sauces made with chopped tomatoes (which are minimally strained), or creamed, crushed or pulped tomatoes. These tomatoes are good for sauces that require long cooking.

CREAMED, CRUSHED AND PULPED TOMATOES
These tomatoes, in cans and jars, have often had seeds and excess liquid removed, so a sauce made from them need not be cooked for so long. *Polpa di pomodoro* is the coarsest version. However, *passata di pomodoro* (often available in bottles) has been liquidised and strained, so it is much thinner, and will need longer heating to evaporate and thicken.

TOMATO CONCENTRATES
Commercially, tomato paste and tomato purée are both concentrates. Tomato purée is virtually what you might produce at home, a purée of tomatoes, with some of the water removed by evaporation. Tomato paste is salted and dehydrated, again to get rid of excess liquid, and to intensify the tomato flavours. As a result, it is much thicker. Both are available in small cans or in tubes. Most brands of paste are a double concentration, but in Italy you can buy triple concentrations and upwards – in Sicily they use a six-times concentrate which they call *strattu*. I love it spread on toast with a little bit of olive oil, like Marmite! These pastes can be – and often should be – diluted with water before use in cooking. If you can find them, sun-dried tomato purée and paste are wonderful.

Other Sauces

Obviously there are other pasta sauces other than meat *ragù* and those made with tomato. Many sauces use some of the cured meats for which Italy is so famous, among them Speck, Parma ham, *guanciale*, salami and pancetta, all of them packed full of savoury flavour. Many sauces are absolutely minimal, some of my favourite pasta dishes are flavoured with nothing more than the juices from a pan in which you have roasted some meat. And never forget the part that various other flavourings play, in meat, tomato, vegetable and seafood sauces: salt and pepper, often oil and vinegar, wine, sometimes cream (although I am not too keen on this, it makes everything taste the same), herbs and spices. Just go easy on these, the Italians never use too much.

VEGETABLE SAUCES
The basis of most pasta sauces is a mixture of vegetables: the *soffritto* consists of onion and/or garlic (or both), celery and carrot, all cubed and fried in oil. Many sauces have a base of tomato, but with other ingredients in them, such as vegetables or seafood. The vegetable sauces of Italy are very seasonal, very simple and very delicious: when fresh peas are in season, they will be used in pasta sauces as well as in soups and risottos (and of course it is all right to use frozen, they are virtually as delicious as fresh). Anything vegetable can be used in a pasta sauce, from green vegetables, to root vegetables (even potatoes), to pulses and fungi. Depending on the vegetable, it will add flavour, texture, and help thicken a sauce, whether whole or mashed down a bit. One of my favourite vegetable flavourings for anything, let alone pasta sauce, is dried *funghi porcini*, dried cep mushrooms. Don't forget to use the liquid you have soaked them in, as it will have become imbued with flavour.

SEAFOOD SAUCES
Fish, shellfish and cephalopods all have a part to play in sauces for pasta. Fish such as red mullet, salmon, monkfish and sardines can all be used to add flavour to pasta, as can commoner shellfish such as mussels and clams, prawns and lobster; when I am in Italy I like to use limpets, sea truffles and sea urchins as well. Squid, octopus and cuttlefish are wonderful in pasta sauces, as is cuttlefish ink. And perhaps the most useful fish of all in making pasta sauces is the anchovy: salted and soaked or filleted in oil, the anchovy melts beautifully into many a pasta sauce, adding inimitable flavour.

PASTA AND THE ITALIAN KITCHEN

In the Italian kitchen, simplicity reigns. There is a basic larder of foodstuffs – all of them of the best affordable quality – and fresh foods are shopped for every day. There are few complicated machines or tools, and a minimum of kitchen aids. Italian food is not complicated to cook, so it does not need complicated preparations. Here I give you a few ideas about the basics you might need for all your pasta-making, cooking and enjoying.

The Larder

As Italian cooking is based on fresh ingredients, there are not many items you will need to keep in stock on a permanent basis. But I like the idea of always having something on hand with which to cook an impromptu meal for friends – pasta, the subject of this book, is the handiest of all in this instance – so I must admit to having quite an extensive larder!

PASTA

I keep probably far too many varieties of pasta – often I am testing them in combination with a new sauce – but I would suggest that you have at least four in your larder. It is handy to have a packet of *pasta per brodo*, some short dried pasta for use in soups: something like stelline or tubettini, for instance, or orzo. I would always have a packet of spaghetti – it is my favourite – but linguine would also be good. I like to have a packet of larger-shaped dried pasta as well, something like pennoni or conchiglie, and I would have a packet of egg tagliatelle nests too. Having these readily available means that you can always knock something up for a quick lunch or supper. Keep an eye on the sell-by dates: pasta lasts a long time, but it can lose flavour with age.

FLOUR

If you plan to make your own pasta at home – and I hope this book will inspire you to do so – you will need to buy some Italian '00' flour. This is extra fine, finer than typical plain flour, although the latter will do at a pinch. If you plan to make some Puglian pasta, you will need to buy some durum wheat semolina flour. Good supermarkets – and the internet – will be able to supply both of these flours.

OILS AND VINEGARS

These will be vital in making sauces for pastas. Most Italian kitchens will have at least three oils: firstly a seed oil, like sunflower, is good for basic frying; secondly, a good olive oil, also for frying, when the wonderful sweetness of olive is required; and lastly, a very good-quality extra virgin olive oil, for making dressings, and for that last-minute drizzle, which adds so much flavour to many a soup or pasta dish. (And I must admit to a luxury oil, truffle, which is wonderful used in the occasional pasta sauce.) As for vinegars, I would have a good red wine vinegar – preferably made from Chianti – a good white wine vinegar, and a not-too-old balsamic.

TOMATOES

I talk about these elsewhere (see pages 22–23), but I would always recommend keeping at least a couple of cans of whole, crushed or chopped tomatoes in your pasta larder, with perhaps a jar of good passata and a small can of tomato paste.

SALT AND PEPPER

These are probably the most used flavour enhancers in all cooking, particularly salt. Salt was the first preserving agent used by man, and is still used in that role in Italy, in preserving fish, capers and in the many pork products. Italian salt is produced mainly in Trapani, Sicily, and parts of Sardinia, from salt pans: flat areas

are flooded with sea water, then the sun evaporates the water. I would always use coarse sea salt, both in cooking and as a topping (for focaccia for instance).

Peppercorns, black, white and green, are the fruit of a vine grown in India, Vietnam and Indonesia. Black and white peppercorns are used a great deal in Italian cooking: in stocks, to season (but lightly), in salamis and on hams. The most important thing to remember about pepper is to buy good peppercorns, and you must also grind them only as needed, for they will lose heat and flavour if ground too long in advance.

HERBS AND SPICES
The Italians use surprisingly few dried herbs, although fresh basil, parsley, sage, mint and rosemary are always recurring in my shopping lists and in my recipes. But once again, we use them sparingly, not generously. Spices were once used widely in early Italian cuisine, and we seem to be taking to them again now (see my recipe for curried red mullet on page 131).

Chillies, however, have been a constant throughout the centuries, ever since their introduction from the Americas in the 16th century. They are used fresh and dried, particularly in the south of the country, where they flourish in the warm sun. Capers, another vital Italian spice flavouring, come from the north and west as well, principally from two islands to the north and west of Sicily, Lipari and Pantelleria. They can be found bottled in salt or in brine; I prefer the former, although they do need to be desalted before use.

GARLIC AND ONIONS
These are much loved in Italian cooking, and in particular in many pasta sauces. Fresh of course, they will be of the best quality – have you ever seen an Italian housewife sniffing and prodding a head of garlic to check its quality before buying? Italy has several special types of onion, such as the onion of Tropea – sweet in flavour, long in shape, and a brilliant red in colour – but mild red or white onions or even shallots would do instead.

FUNGHI PORCINI

I am passionate about fungi in general and about *funghi porcini*, or ceps, in particular. The latter are dried, and are an essential in your pasta larder: rehydrated in water, they can add extraordinary flavour to many a sauce. *Porcini* stock cubes are also available now, in better delis and supermarkets. Keep opened packets in the fridge.

ANCHOVIES

Preserved anchovies are a major flavour enhancer of many Italian dishes. You will find fillets in cans, preserved in oil or whole fish in jars, preserved in salt. I prefer the latter, though they are fiddly to debone and desalt, but the others are less so and are still very tasty.

PRESERVED MEATS

The Italians have a multitude of preserved, salted or air-cured meats and salami that are very useful as a stand-by snack and, inevitably, in pasta sauce making. I always have some pancetta, our Italian bacon, which I freeze in those packets of cubes, or buy sliced from the delicatessen. In days gone by I would have had *lardo*, a type of very tasty salted and air-cured lard or pork fat, an ideal addition to the oil, garlic and onion fried at the beginning of a delicious pasta sauce. Another similar meat is Speck, the Tyrolean counterpart to *lardo*.

CHEESES

Italy has a wealth of glorious cheeses, many of which are used in pasta sauces, pasta fillings and as a final flavouring for a finished dish. The soft cheeses such as ricotta, mascarpone and mozzarella are obviously not standard larder items: you would have to buy them specially for a dish, chill them and use them quickly. Hard Italian cheeses will last longer, and my pasta kitchen would never be without Parmesan or, second-best but still delicious, Grana Padano or pecorino

(Sardo or Romano). These are the prime cheeses to add wonderful flavour to a stuffed pasta filling, or to grate onto a dish of pasta at the end. Keep these cheeses wrapped in foil in the fridge.

Pasta-making Equipment

You don't really need to have any special equipment to make your pasta and you will probably already possess many of the tools you will find most useful. I am thinking about a wooden chopping board, a good long wooden rolling pin, a large steel saucepan (with a lid) for cooking the pasta, and a large colander through which to drain it. Ideally the pan should be larger at the base than at the top: this enables the water the pasta is cooked in to remain at the same temperature, thus helping the pasta to cook perfectly. Other helpful items you may already have are a grater for cheese and a pasta scoop or spoon, or tongs.

If you are keen on making your own pasta at home, you might need a larger board than the one you already have, and of course you might want to buy a manual pasta-making machine such as 'Imperia'; these range in price according to function. A pastry-cutting wheel will be useful for some of the shapes, while specialist shops often sell ravioli wheels.

You could buy a *raviolatrice*, which is like a rectangular grid over which you place one length of pasta. You press the pasta carefully down into the square ravioli moulds, then fill the moulds with some of your filling. Then you cover the moulds with another length of rectangular pasta. Roll over this with your rolling pin, which will cut the dough into perfect ravioli shapes. Remove each raviolo carefully and place on a floured surface, ready for the filling.

MAKING FRESH PASTA

Most people might think that making fresh pasta is a major task. Nothing could be further from the truth! Even the equipment can be reduced to an absolute minimum: all you really need is a knife, a rolling pin and a surface to work on. (You might choose to go down the pasta-machine route – that's even quicker!) The time involved when making by hand is probably about 30 minutes at first, but you will get much quicker with practice. The ingredients you will need per person are 100g of Italian '00' flour, a free-range egg, and a little water if the egg is small. If making a non-egg pasta, like that from Puglia, you will need to use fine durum wheat semolina flour and some water (no egg). The rest is elbow grease and passion.

What you want to obtain is a soft dough, which will be rolled out with your rolling pin to the desired thickness – this varies (page 30) – and then cut with a knife. The freshly made pasta is used to make all sorts of pasta shapes and lengths: from capelli d'angelo, tagliolini, tagliatelle, maltagliati, stracci, to all sorts of stuffed pastas like cappelletti, tortellini, tortelli, ravioli, ravioloni, cannelloni, as well as lasagne, farfalle and any other regional shapes such as passatelli or spätzle. The only things you can't make at home are the extruded shapes you would buy dried: the tubular pastas like penne and the round lengths such as spaghetti, etc.

You can vary your homemade pasta in a number of ways. You can mix spinach, beetroot, black cuttlefish ink, cocoa and powdered *porcini* into the fresh egg pasta to achieve whatever colour and flavour you may want. And you could make a chestnut pasta, or a gluten-free pasta: simply replace some or all of the flour in the recipe with the chosen flour.

You can probably make enough of your own pasta to store some. Cut the pasta into whatever shapes you want, leave it to dry completely on a clean tea towel or a lightly floured surface, then pack it very carefully into an airtight bag or container. Wind long strands such as tagliatelle into nests while the pasta is still pliable: this will help protect them from breakage later. The pasta will keep in the fridge for two to three days, or you can freeze it for up to six months. If freezing, wrap it in clingfilm or foil first, then defrost in the normal way (not in a microwave!).

Pasta Fresca all'Uovo
{ Fresh Egg Pasta }

This is the basic recipe, which will make enough pasta to feed about four people. I said earlier that you need roughly 100g flour and an egg per person, in which case you might think the recipe below would serve only three people. However, if you do your maths – the 300g flour plus three eggs (roughly 50g each) – it all adds up to 450g, which is plenty of pasta for four people. The method is shown on pages 30–1.

You can vary this fresh egg pasta recipe by adding other colouring ingredients. When you add one of these, you will have to be careful to keep a balance – leave out an egg perhaps, or add more flour – just to keep the proportions even, and avoid too wet a mixture.

MAKES ABOUT 450G

300g Italian '00' flour
3 medium eggs
a pinch of salt

{1}   {2}   {3}

By hand

Sift the flour onto a work surface, forming it into a volcano-shaped mound with a well in the centre {1}. Break the eggs into this well and add the salt {2}. (Add the colouring ingredient now if using.) Incorporate the eggs into the flour with a fork and your hands, gradually drawing the flour into the egg mixture until it forms a coarse paste {3+4}. Add a little more flour if the mixture is too soft or sticky – or a little water if the mixture is too dry. Using your knife (or a spatula), scrape up any stray pieces of dough.

Before kneading the dough clean your hands and the work surface. Lightly flour the work surface, and start to knead the dough with the heel of one hand as you might bread dough. Work the dough for 10–15 minutes until the consistency is smooth and elastic {5}. If you have dough sticking to your fingers, rub your hands with some flour. Wrap the dough in clingfilm or foil and leave it to rest for at least half an hour.

When ready to (rock and) roll, lightly flour your work surface again, and your rolling pin. Gently roll the dough out from the middle of the dough, rolling away from you to take the thickness away from the centre, and rotating it in quarter turns {6}. As you roll, stretch the dough using the rolling pin, and turn the sheet of rolled dough over every now and again in order to keep it all even. Keep everything well floured to avoid sticking.

The thickness of your dough will depend on the pasta shape you are using: anything from 0.5mm to 3mm. In general the larger the shape, the thicker the rolled pasta: lasagne is generally quite thick, but then again mandilli de sea, which can be as large in surface area as lasagne, has to be very thin indeed. The pasta for filled pastas has to be thin, because there is so much folding and sealing, you don't want great lumps of thick pasta; and the more delicate the filling, the thinner the pasta casing. You will have to practise, and use your common sense, and follow the recipes! Pasta can be quite tricky – but to encourage you, not all Italians know as much as you do now!

If you are making filled pasta go straight ahead and incorporate the filling as in the chosen recipe, while the pasta dough is still malleable. This is better than leaving the cut pieces for a while, when a moist filling might seep through the pasta or indeed perforate it. Dust the shapes with semolina flour to help prevent sticking.

If you are making flat pasta or shapes, cut them out and leave on a clean tea towel to dry for about half an hour before cooking or storing. Coil long pasta into nests first, as this makes the pasta easier to handle once you come to cook it.

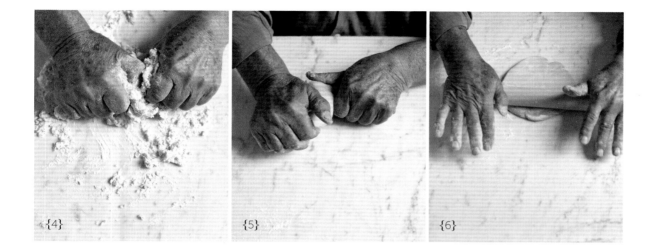

{4} {5} {6}

By machine

Blend all the ingredients together in a food processeor until you have a homogeneous dough. Lift out, and 'knead' the dough by putting it through your pasta machine. Divide the dough into pieces (follow the machine instructions). Put one part of the dough through the steel rollers with a maximum aperture of about 1cm. Repeat this with the same piece of rolled dough, while reducing the size of the aperture between the two rollers. Being forced through a smaller gap, the pasta dough is worked more, becomes thinner, and more silky. The ultimate width of 1–2mm produces a long band of pasta of about 15–18cm wide. Cut into lengths of about 30cm.

You then use the machine cutting tool to make lengths of tagliatelle, say (the widest cut), or tagliolini (the smallest cut). Mix in a little flour, roll the strands into nests, and spread out on a cloth to dry as before.

Coloured pasta

PASTA VERDE { Green Pasta }
Add 75g well-drained, puréed cooked spinach to the basic ingredients, leaving out 1 egg.

PASTA PURPUREA { Purple Pasta }
Add 4 tbsp beetroot juice to the basic ingredients, leaving out 1 egg.

PASTA ARANCIONE { Orange Pasta }
Add 4 tbsp carrot juice (freshly made or bought) to the basic ingredients, leaving out 1 egg.

PASTA ROSSA { Red Pasta }
Add $1\frac{1}{2}$ tbsp tomato purée to the basic ingredients.

PASTA NERA { Black Pasta }
Add 1–2 tsp cuttlefish ink to the basic ingredients.

PASTA DI PORCINI { Mushroom Pasta }
Dry dried *porcini* further by placing on a baking sheet in a low oven until really crisp. When cold, reduce to a powder in a spice grinder. Add 2 tbsp to the basic ingredients.

PASTA DI CIOCCOLATO { Chocolate Pasta }
Add 2 tbsp good cocoa powder to the basic ingredients.

Eggless pasta

Allowing 100g durum wheat semolina flour and 40ml water per person, mix together until firm but malleable. Knead well and leave to rest for at least 20 minutes before using.

Shaping *Pasta Lunga*
{ Long Pasta }

Long pasta shapes are probably the best known of all pastas: spaghetti and lasagne (this counts as 'long') are to be found in most storecupboards. The easiest way to make the long and delicate shapes such as capelli d'angelo, tagliolini, fettuccine and spaghetti alla chitarra is with a machine. But you can still successfully make some of the long shapes by hand and it is probably less time-consuming because there is not so much washing up!

If using a machine, it will make your pasta as thin or thick as you like. It is more difficult by hand. But in general, the thickness of the rolled-out pasta dough should match the shape you are cutting: the width and height should be about the same. But don't attempt this with pappardelle – you don't want them to be 2cm thick!

Step by step

For the following five pasta types, fold the sheet of pasta dough into a wide, flat sausage {1}, dusting abundantly with flour.

PAPPARDELLE
Cut the rolled pasta into 2cm wide strips.

FETTUCCINE
Cut the rolled pasta into 6–7mm wide strips.

TAGLIATELLE
Cut the rolled pasta into 5mm wide strips {2}.

TAGLIOLINI/TAJERIN
Cut the rolled pasta into 3mm wide strips.

CAPELLI D'ANGELO
Cut the rolled pasta into 1–2mm wide strips.

For the following pasta types, simply roll out the pasta as described.

MACCHERONI/SPAGHETTI ALLA CHITARRA
Roll out the pasta to 2mm thick sheets, then cut into 2mm wide strips.

BIGOLI { square not round }
Roll out the pasta to 4mm thick sheets, then cut into 4mm wide strips.

PINCI/PICI { a durum wheat semolina pasta from Tuscany, usually made by machine }
Take a little piece of dough and roll it out by hand to a long sausage shape on your work surface. It will probably be uneven, but that will add to its charm.

In each case, shake out the strips of pasta {3} and then, holding the pasta at one end, wind it into a nest to dry.

LASAGNE/RAVIOLO APERTO
Cut a trimmed oblong of pasta into large squares or oblongs – you could use a serrated pastry wheel for a different look – and stack, separated with greaseproof paper, to dry.

MANDILLI DE SEA
The same idea as lasagne, just roll the pasta dough a little thinner.

Shaping *Pasta Corta*
{ Short Pasta }

Short pasta includes shapes such as farfalle, fusilli and garganelli, which are cut and formed from flattened, rolled-out dough, but also shapes such as orecchiette and gnocchetti sardi, which are made by shaping balls of pasta with your fingers. Garganelli, which are made by hand, can be substituted for penne, which obviously can only be made by machine. The very simplest short pasta shape, gnocchi, is made from simply slicing a sausage-like length of pasta dough. To make any short pasta shape ribbed, simply roll it against a butter-pat or other similar ridged surface – the tines of a fork are useful as well!

Please take on board that homemade short pasta will never look like the machined perfection of shop-bought.

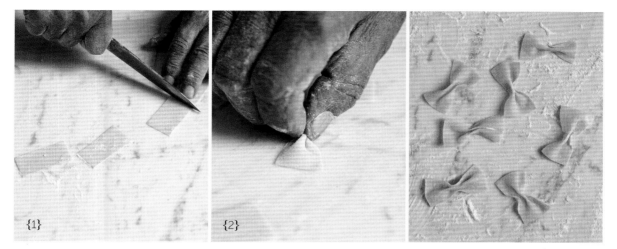

{1} {2}

{ Farfalle }

Step by step, rolling-pin-rolled dough

Start with a flattened or rolled-out piece of pasta dough of about 1mm thick. Trim the edges of the dough with a plain or serrated wheel. Divide the dough into two oblongs roughly 12 x 36cm. Next, divide the two oblongs into neat squares of pasta of approximately 6 x 6cm.

FARFALLE

Divide your squares into halves to form oblongs using a knife or serrated pastry wheel {1}. To form the bow or butterfly shape, pinch the oblong of dough in the centre {2}.

FUSILLI

Cut the 6cm square into four long strips. Firmly twine a strip of pasta on to a thickish knitting needle to form a spiral {1}. Take out the needle and leave the fusilli to dry {2}. (Commercial fusilli are extruded in many different ways: some are rolled round a needle, some are used flat.) You could also roll the strips of dough by hand into little sausage shapes before wrapping them round the needle.

{ Fusilli }

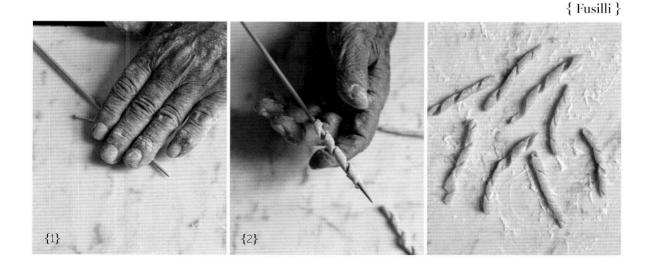

{1} {2}

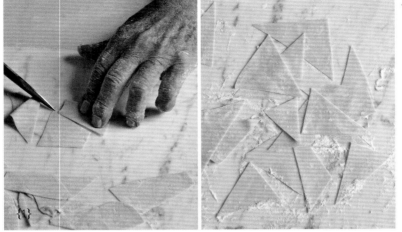

{ Maltagliati }

MALTAGLIATI

Take a large oblong of pasta and cut it arbitrarily using a plain pastry wheel {1}.

QUADRUCCI

These are flat squares of pasta. Roll out the pasta dough, by hand or machine, to as thin as possible. Cut into bands 2cm wide, as if making pappardelle. Put one band on top of each other, using a little flour in between layers to prevent sticking {1}. Cut now through the layers into 2cm squares {2}.

GARGANELLI

Take a 6cm square of pasta, moisten one side with water and roll firmly, and at a slight angle, around the end of a wooden spoon. Then roll over a ridged butter-pat, before removing the spoon handle.

BRANDELLI

The simplest pasta shape ever, and one that I invented. Just tear a piece of rolled-out dough at random to form uneven pieces. (*Brandelli* means 'in tatters'! Other similar shapes are stracci or mandilli de sea.)

{ Quadrucci }

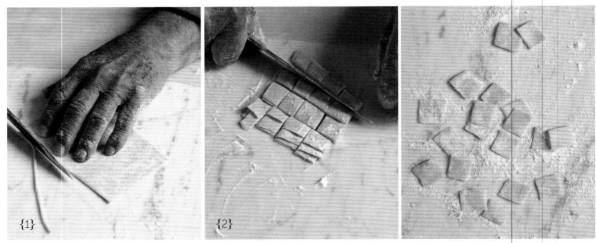

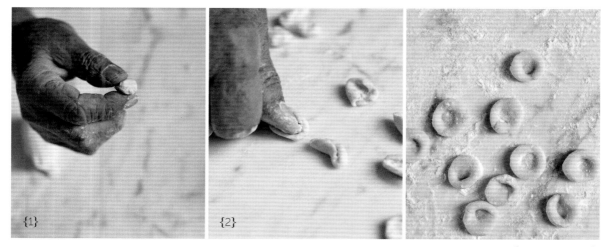

Step by step, hand-rolled dough

These pastas involve taking pieces of dough to form shapes by hand, without the use of a rolling pin.

TROFIE

Roll out a small piece of dough into a sausage shape of around 3mm in diameter. Cut into 3–4cm lengths. Roll these lengths between your hands on your work surface until extended a bit, then twist the ends in different directions to get an uneven spiral.

ORECCHIETTE

Roll out a piece of dough into a sausage shape of around 1cm in diameter and 30cm in length. Cut the length of dough into small 1cm pieces, then form each into an even ball {1}. To make the orecchiette, press on the ball of dough with your thumb, at the same time pushing it away from you slightly so that the dough curls into a shell, or ear, shape {2}.

GNOCCHETTI SARDI/MALLOREDDUS

Make a small sausage of pasta of about 2.5cm in length. Press the pasta on to a ridged butter-pat. Press and push it firmly to form a small ridged sausage.

Pasta Fresca Ripiena
{ Filled Fresh Pasta }

Filled pastas are more typical of the northern parts of Italy. (In the south, 'fillings' would probably be accompanied by lasagne.) In the regions of Emilia-Romagna, Lombardy, Piedmont and Liguria, you will find an amazing number of filled pastas, some the same, some different, some with similar fillings, some with a multitude of shapes, all with names sometimes the same, sometimes different! These anomalies have existed for a long time, and there is no getting round them. For instance, agnolotti, the ravioli of Piedmont, can be square, rectangular, round or half-moon shaped. Tortelli, the filled pasta of Emilia-Romagna, can be square, round or half-moon shaped. Some tortelli are rectangular... Confused? Yes, we all are, even the Italians...

Filled or stuffed pasta may sound difficult and fiddly to make, but it's really quite easy – and it's so delicious. There is absolutely no comparison between what you can make at home and what you can buy in a shop. You can experiment with different fillings, for instance, and you can play with sizes. The traditional basic shapes of filled pasta are few, but you can create interest by making them large or small. For instance ravioli are usually 2cm square, but you can make raviolini which are smaller, or ravioloni which are larger. (The same linguistic rules apply to other shapes: tortelli, tortellini, tortelloni etc.) Always bear in mind that the amount of filling used should be in good relation to the size of the pasta.

When making filled pastas, you must take care that the filling is not too moist, as this tends to soften the pasta, which may burst while cooking. When stacking and storing stuffed pastas, put a little durum wheat semolina flour between them to prevent them sticking together. And always use water to help the layers of pasta to stick to each other; many recipes specify beaten egg, but this will cook to form a layer of its own, adding to the thickness of the pasta, which you don't want.

RAVIOLI/AGNOLOTTI

Cut out a piece of pasta dough, 37 x 24cm. Cut out another piece of pasta dough, marginally larger than the first. Dot the smaller piece evenly with filling. (If making the traditional 2cm squares, use about $\frac{1}{2}$ teaspoon filling at 2cm intervals: you should get about 15.) Moisten around the edges of the filling portions with water to aid sealing. Place the larger, second piece of pasta over the first {1}, pressing down around the piles of filling to push out any air.

Alternatively, you could have one large sheet of pasta instead of two. Dot the filling along one side, moisten as above, and then fold the other half over. Divide the ravioli into separate pieces using a serrated pastry or ravioli wheel {2}. (Or you could just use a *raviolatrice*, as opposite, and see page 26.)

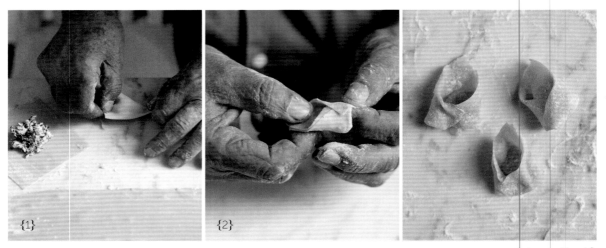

CAPPELLETTI

You can start off with squares or rounds of pasta. (Cappellacci are made in the same way, but are larger.) Place small 2.5cm squares of pasta on your work surface, and put a teaspoon or so of filling in the centre, or slightly to one side of the centre. Fold into a triangle, pushing out all the air around the filling and pressing the edges to seal {1}. Bring the two widest points of the triangle together, pinching them firmly so they hold {2}. Turn the pointed end of the triangle up at an angle to complete the shape.

Alternatively, put 8–9cm circles of pasta on your work surface. Place a level teaspoon of the filling on each circle and fold over, sealing the edge with a little water {below}. Then roll the semi-circle of sealed pasta into a sausage and bend it round to join the ends together, pressing the seal down on the work surface with your thumb {below}.

TORTELLONI/TORTELLINI/ANOLINI

For tortelloni, make as round cappelletti, with circles of 6cm in diameter. For tortellini, use 5cm squares or rounds of pasta. For anolini, use 3cm squares or rounds of pasta. (I can't make the latter, my fingers are too big!)

{ Tortelloni }

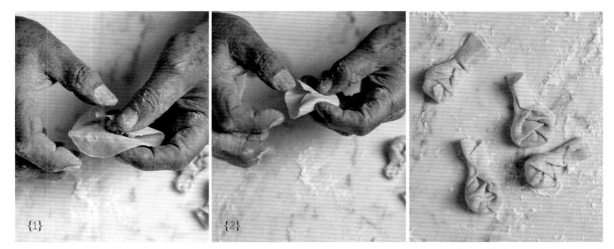

{ Sardinian Culurgiones }

MARUBINI
Cut into circles of whatever size you want, but usually fairly small, about 5cm. Put the filling in the middle of one, moisten the edges, and top with another circle. Seal well. Or make them as you would ravioli, pressing between the piles of filling before cutting. (See page 39.)

AGNOLOTTI DEL PLIN
Make as for ravioli, but in rectangular shapes. Before cutting, pinch between the piles of filling, then cut through the pinched, pleated pasta.

CIALZONS/AGNOLOTTI (FROM FRIULI)
An 8cm circle, folded in half over the filling. The edges are then folded over to seal.

RAVIOLONI
Cut out a piece of pasta about 50 x 25cm, and place dots of filling – more generous than above – at 6–7cm intervals. Moisten as above, top with another piece of pasta, and cut into 6–7cm squares.

PANSÒTI
Very typical of Liguria. Cut pieces of pasta, 5–8cm square, then fold into a triangle over the filling.

ORECCHIONI/TORDELLONI/RAVIOLONI
10cm circles of pasta, folded over the filling.

TORTELLI CON LA CODA/CARAMELLE
An 8cm rectangle of pasta, wrapped around the filling, and twisted at the ends like a boiled sweet. The dough must be rolled very thinly.

CANNELLONI
Take a long strip of trimmed pasta dough, roughly 8 x 15cm. Roll up the filling in the pasta. Moisten the overlapping edges and trim.

SARDINIAN CULURGIONES
Cut out circles 8cm in diameter, and put one in your non-working hand. Place the filling off centre, towards the bottom of your hand. With your thumb, pinch a fold of dough over from the bottom to cover the filling {1}, and then fold over alternately from left and right to give a pleated effect {2}. Pinch in at the centre as you go, to seal the ravioli, and seal the top with a final pinch. The end product looks slightly pear-shaped.

THE PASTA CODE

Cooking

HOW MUCH PASTA?

For small portions, for a starter, allow 50g dried or 90g fresh pasta per person. For normal portions, for a lunch with a salad, say, cook about 70–80g dried or 100–110g fresh pasta per person. For larger portions – for growing teenagers or athletes – I would use from 100–110g dried or 130–150g fresh pasta per person. Everything depends, of course, on the quality and shape of the pasta, and on appetite!

THE SAUCEPAN

The pan in which you boil the pasta must be large – broad as well as high – because you will be using a lot of water. Ideally the pan should be larger at the base than at the top, which helps retain the water temperature. You also need a lid: you have to cover the pan briefly once the pasta has been added, in order to bring the water back to boiling point as quickly as possible. The lid is then taken off during the pasta cooking.

THE WATER…

Use 1 litre water per 100g pasta. You need at least this amount because of the starch the pasta gives out in cooking. If there were too small a quantity of water, the dissolving starch would be re-absorbed by the pasta. The water must be boiling vigorously when the pasta is added.

…OR STOCK

You could use a good homemade chicken stock instead of water to cook fine long pasta or small shapes, which will make the pasta taste better; for many soups or minestroni, this is the standard way of cooking the pasta content. Use stock in the same proportions as water, and bring it to the boil before adding the pasta.

THE SALT

Add 10g salt per litre of water just before it comes to the boil and the pasta is added. Use coarse sea salt if possible. A stock, if previously unseasoned, will need much the same salt quantity as water, but do be careful as of course you are probably going to be drinking the stock.

THE COOKING

When the water comes to the boil, add small pasta shapes all at once, and stir after 20–30 seconds. Cover until the water comes back to the boil. Remove the lid and cook the pasta for from 2–3 minutes for fresh homemade and up to 18–20 minutes for dried non-egg pasta (always follow the directions on the packet), most Pugliese pastas and some dried filled pastas. (Generally speaking, dried pasta takes twice the cooking time allowed for fresh.) If you are cooking longer strands, put them into the boiling water in bunches, never breaking the strands. If your pot is tall enough, as the pasta at the bottom softens, push it down with a wooden fork until fully covered with water. Stir as above, and cook for the appropriate length of time.

ADDING OIL

You don't need to add oil to a pan of pasta unless you are cooking pasta sheets like lasagne, which might stick together: to prevent this, add the sheets one by one to the oiled water so that the oil coats the lasagne surface. Otherwise, to prevent pasta sticking together, you should stir once or twice during cooking, using a wooden fork.

THE AL DENTE TEST

This can never be precise: *al dente* means literally 'to the tooth', which suggests not stiff, not soft, but pliable and cooked through, with no chalky core at the centre. Test one or two pieces of pasta towards the end of cooking to see if it is to your liking: remove a piece or a strand with your wooden fork, and cool a little before tasting. Most Italians like it *al dente*, still with that light resistance to the tooth; the Neapolitans like their pasta with so much resistance that the pasta strands can spring off the plate (in local dialect, *fuienni*)! Many other people like it much softer, but please don't cook it for too long, as it become slightly indigestible, giving you a feeling of weight in your stomach.

DRAINING THE PASTA

Have ready a large colander in the sink, into which you drain the pasta. (Save a few tablespoons of the pasta cooking water; this could be useful if your pasta sauce is too dry or too thick.) Never rinse the pasta, whether with cold or hot water, as this will wash away too much of the starch coating. If you are cooking long pasta, you could lift this from the pan using pasta tongs and then return to the pan after most of the water has been drained off.

Serving and Eating

HEATING THE PLATES

Preheat both the serving dish, if using, and the individual plates. Italians like deep plates for pasta, such as you might use for soup.

DRESSING THE PASTA WITH SAUCE

Always have your pasta sauce prepared by the time the pasta is cooked. This must be speedy, as pasta pieces will stick together if not dressed quickly. There are several ways of dressing the pasta with sauce. You could return the drained pasta to its saucepan, or place in a preheated bowl, to keep it warm. You could add a little olive oil or butter before the sauce, and stir, but I normally use just a little of the cooking water. Add some of the sauce, and toss the pasta to coat each piece. Divide the pasta between heated bowls or plates, and top each portion with a little more of the sauce. Another, simpler, way is

to put the drained pasta in the saucepan with the sauce, and mixing in the pan before serving out. But remember that the pasta mustn't be swimming in sauce.

DRESSING THE PASTA WITH CHEESE

If necessary, add freshly grated Parmesan, pecorino or Caciocavallo cheese. (Aged cheeses are usually better.) Put some on top of the pasta and sauce in the serving bowl, and have some in a separate bowl for extra helpings. But don't use cheese with fish pasta dishes, these might benefit instead from the flavour of a little stream of extra virgin olive oil.

EATING THE PASTA

Serve the pasta hot, and if it is long, eat only with a fork: lift a few strings of pasta from the plate with your fork, make a little space on the side, pin the fork down and start to twirl as if using a screwdriver. (Collecting a few strings only avoids you winding up with too big a mouthful.) The worst offence against pasta-eating etiquette is cutting long pasta with a knife, in order to eat it with a spoon. Using a spoon as well as a fork comes a near second... you should only use a spoon when eating soups or soupy pasta dishes. Try also not to suck strings into your mouth: only babies are usually allowed to do this, although the great Sophia Loren, in her book on Italian cooking, expressed a liking for this method!

MOPPING UP THE PLATE

There should really never be any sauce left at the bottom of an emptied pasta plate. But there are some Italians who commit the ultimate pasta faux pas by cleaning their plates with a piece of bread. This tastes good, however, and is known as *la scarpetta* little shoes.

KEEP ANY LEFTOVERS

Never throw away any leftover plain pasta or sauced pasta. There will always be something you can do with it, and I will give you a few ideas (see page 188).

PART TWO

THE PASTA RECIPES

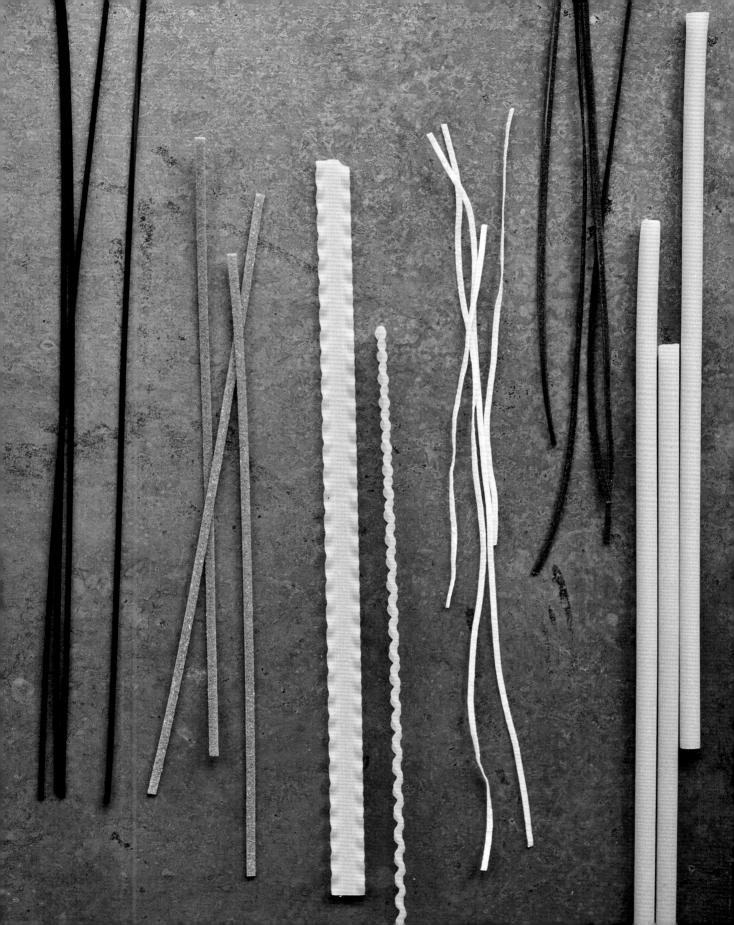

PASTA IN BRODO

PASTA IN SOUPS

I have always liked soups, a fondness which started in the nursery, when my mother would cook us soups based on cabbage or other vegetables, with rice or pasta. These were warm, filling and delicious and, at the same time, very nutritious. As an adult, I lived abroad, but whenever I came home to visit her, she always seemed to be waiting with a saucepan of *pastina in brodo*. This comforting broth, strongly reduced as consommé, brings back such strong memories of home, and of my mother herself.

Soups in Italy are roughly divided into various types. *Zuppa* is usually a broth containing ingredients which have not been liquidised, and often has a slice of bread at the bottom. A *passata* is a *zuppa* which has been liquidised (often called a *crema* as well). A *minestra* is a soup normally based on broth and green vegetables. (A *minestrone* is a big *minestra*!) Italian soups of any kind – whether of meat, fish or vegetable, fresh or leftover – are eaten mostly in the evening as part of a light meal, perhaps followed by a herb omelette and salad. Many soups call for a delicious homemade stock, but often water will do just as well (and, perhaps surprisingly, I am not averse to using good-quality stock cubes or powder instead of stock, should the need arise).

But we are talking here of soups involving pasta in one form or other, and many special soup pastas are available. These are very small, and include acini di pepe, alfabeto or lettere, ditalini and orzo. They are all, almost without exception, made from durum wheat semolina, in a machine, extruded at high pressure through tiny dies, and then cut and dried. Some *pasta per brodo* may be made with egg, and some may be made from a flour containing no gluten, to cater for those with coeliac disease or wheat intolerance.

Adding pasta to soup obviously helps to thicken it, but it also adds a very nice texture. If you haven't got *pasta per brodo*, you could always break up larger pieces of dried pasta, lasagne or pappardelle for instance. You could also break up dried tagliolini or capelli d'angelo to use in an intense chicken broth – the Italian version of chicken noodle soup!

Pastina in Brodo
{ Small Pasta in Broth }

SERVES 4

200g small dried eggless pasta, like farfalline,
    semi di melone, alfabeto, conchigliette
salt and pepper, to taste
20g unsalted butter
50g Parmesan, freshly grated
1 tbsp chopped fresh flat-leaf parsley

BEEF STOCK (MAKES ABOUT 3 LITRES)
1kg stewing beef in one piece, plus a few beef bones
4 litres water
salt
2 carrots, peeled and cut into pieces
1 onion, peeled and halved
2–3 celery stalks, roughly chopped
4 bay leaves
1 tbsp black peppercorns

To make the stock, immerse the meat in the water in a
large saucepan, add a pinch of salt and bring to the boil.
Skim off the froth and add the remaining ingredients.
Bring back to the boil, cover with the lid, and allow to
simmer for 2–3 hours. Remove the meat and keep aside
if using in another dish. Strain the stock, and discard
everything else. When the stock has cooled, remove any
solidified fat. Chill to use within a day or two, or freeze.
Taste for seasoning before use.

For the soup, bring 600ml of the stock to the boil in a
large saucepan. Add the pasta, taste for salt, and cook
until tender, from 5–8 minutes, depending on the type of
pasta. Season to taste.

Add the butter to taste, allow it to melt, then serve
the soup in hot bowls, sprinkled with the Parmesan
and parsley.

ALTERNATIVES

For a lighter version of this classic northern Italian soup, try
using homemade chicken stock (see page 55). Whole or
broken-up capelli d'angelo can be substituted for the usual
pasta per brodo, and you could add some finely chopped
parsley or chives as you serve.

Pasta e Patate
{ Pasta and Potato Soup }

SERVES 4

300g fresh eggless pasta (see page 31)
100g lardo, or the fatty part of pancetta or prosciutto
2 garlic cloves, peeled and finely chopped
2 tbsp olive oil
about 400g semi-floury potatoes,
    peeled and cubed
the leafy tops of a head of celery,
    finely chopped
200g celeriac, peeled and finely chopped
1.5 litres water or chicken stock (see page 55)
salt and pepper, to taste

Roll out the pasta, by hand or machine, to 2mm thick.
Cut into strips 5cm long and 2.5cm wide.

Fry a *soffritto* of the fat, garlic and oil together for a few
minutes, then add the potatoes, celery leaves and celeriac.
Fry for a few more minutes, stirring, then add the water
or stock. Cook gently until everything is soft, about
15 minutes. Add salt to taste and abundant pepper.

Add the pasta, and continue to cook until the pasta is
soft, about 6–7 minutes – you don't want *al dente* here.
Neither do you need Parmesan, as the flavour is already
so good.

ALTERNATIVE

The celeriac, which is my addition to this classic and
extremely filling and satisfying dish of my mother's, can be
replaced with the same quantity of Jerusalem artichoke for
a different flavour.

Orecchiette con Broccoli e Cozze

{ Ear-shaped Pasta with Broccoli and Mussels }

This is a dish typical of the Pugliese coast, particularly the port of Bari, and any available shellfish can be used. The sauce is usually made with *broccoli di rapa* or *cime di rapa*, turnip tops. These are not generally found other than in Italy, and the easiest alternative is little broccoli florets (the calabrese type) or purple sprouting broccoli tops. The dish can be served as a starter – in small portions! – or as a very nice lunch.

SERVES 4

350g dried orecchiette pasta
salt and pepper, to taste
300g tips of purple sprouting broccoli
75ml extra virgin olive oil
2 garlic cloves, peeled and finely chopped
1 fresh hot red chilli, chopped, to taste
4 cherry tomatoes, halved
3 tbsp dry white wine
1kg largish mussels, cleaned

ALTERNATIVES

Instead of the mussels, you could use clams, which will need a slightly shorter cooking time. You could also use gnocchetti sardi or penne instead of the orecchiette. If you can find them, red or green orecchioni would look very pretty with the mussels and broccoli. Pugliese orecchiette are made with both Italian '00' flour and durum wheat semolina, which makes them very interesting in texture, requiring slightly longer cooking than other small dried pasta types. Although often handmade in Puglia, you can also find dried orecchiette in packets in good delicatessens.

Cook the pasta in plenty of boiling salted water for 10 minutes or until nearly *al dente* (taste a piece!). After this time, add the broccoli to the pan with the pasta, and cook them together for another 5–6 minutes. Drain the pasta and broccoli.

Meanwhile, heat most of the oil with the garlic and chilli (use as much or as little as you like) in a large pan for a minute or so. Then add the tomatoes, the wine and the cleaned mussels. Put the lid on and steam for about 8–10 minutes, but it very much depends on size (take a look). The mussels will soon open in the heat, releasing their delicious juices. Remove the pan from the heat and pull some of the mussels from their shells. Put the meat back in the sauce and discard the extra shells. Sauté the mussels a little to allow them to absorb the flavours, adding the remaining extra virgin olive oil. Don't add any salt as the mussel juices are salty, and the pasta has already been salted but do taste for pepper.

Put the pasta and broccoli into the sauce in the pan, and mix. A little brothy, this pasta should be served in deep plates, and can be eaten with a spoon.

Tortellini in Brodo

{ Small Stuffed Pasta in Broth }

Without doubt, the most genuine recipe in the region of Emilia-Romagna is their brothy soup, which is served as a first course even at the most elegant meals. It is possible to use factory-made tortellini, but the best are homemade. The Emiliani take quite some time to produce these fresh for special occasions. Tortellini isn't just used in soup, it can also be eaten with a tomato sauce or even with ham and cream.

SERVES 4

½ recipe fresh egg pasta (see page 29)
600ml very good beef stock (see page 47)
salt and pepper, to taste
50g Parmesan, freshly grated

FILLING
200g leftover roast beef or veal, minced
10 Brussels sprouts, softly boiled, very
    finely chopped
½ tsp each of freshly grated nutmeg and
    ground cinnamon
1 medium egg
30g Parmesan, freshly grated

ALTERNATIVES

You could use cappellacci instead of the tortellini. Sprinkle with a green leaf, such as parsley, chives or celery leaves.

Make the pasta (see page 30). Roll it out by passing through the rollers of a small pasta machine or with a rolling pin to 1mm thick. Cut into 8cm squares.

Mix together all the ingredients for the filling. Put a little of the mixture in the centre of each pasta square. Fold one corner of the pasta to the other over the filling to make a triangle, and press to seal. Fold the two remaining corners around the little finger and press together: you should have formed a round shape with a belly button. Do the same with all the remaining pasta and filling. (You can make these a day before. If you want to keep them for longer they have to be frozen.)

Bring the stock to the boil. Throw in the tortellini and, when the stock comes back to the boil, cook for 3–4 minutes if fresh, 10 minutes from frozen (and 15 minutes if they are dried from a packet). Taste a tortellino to see if it is ready. Taste the stock for seasoning.

Serve the tortellini and broth in a warmed deep soup plate or bowl, and sprinkle with Parmesan.

Zuppa di Agnello Falso Allarme

{ White Spring Lamb Soup with Small Pasta Tubes }

To glorify what I thought was a wonderful spring day, I created this recipe. However, halfway through, the snow started to come down, turning my garden white. The sunshine was a false alarm, so this soup turned into a recipe to satisfy my wish for winter comfort!

SERVES 4

60ml olive oil
2 onions, peeled and coarsely chopped
1 whole celeriac, peeled and cubed
3 carrots, peeled and cubed
700g lamb neck cutlets
1.5 litres water
2 chicken stock cubes (yes, I do use them
    sometimes!)
1 fresh rosemary sprig
salt and pepper, to taste
250g dried ziti tagliati pasta (or maccheroni)
2 tbsp finely chopped fresh flat-leaf parsley

Pour the oil into a large saucepan and fry the onions for about 5 minutes, then add the celeriac and carrots, and fry for a further 5–6 minutes. Add the lamb, pour over the water and crumble in the stock cubes. Bring to the boil, add the rosemary with some salt and pepper to taste, then cover with the lid and simmer for an hour.

Remove the meat from the pan, and discard the bones. Cut the meat into little chunks, and return to the soup. Add the pasta and cook for a further 8–10 minutes.

Serve hot, sprinkled with parsley.

ALTERNATIVES

You could use sedanini or tubettini, anything small for the soup. If you left out the pasta, and made the soup less liquid, it would make a nice sauce for something like penne.

Tajarin in Brodo con Gnocchetti di Pollo

{ Small Ribbons with Chicken Dumplings in Broth }

Piedmont is famous for its tajarin noodles, which the Piedmontese like to eat with truffle. To make them, you need just a little fresh egg pasta dough (see page 29), which when rolled out can be cut into small irregular ribbons a couple of millimetres wide – it's easy!

SERVES 4

½ recipe fresh egg pasta (see page 29)
a handful of celery leaves (optional)
40g Parmesan, freshly grated
salt and pepper, to taste

CHICKEN STOCK (MAKES ABOUT 3 LITRES)
1.75kg raw chicken pieces
1 bouquet garni, or a sprig of parsley
    and a bay leaf
4 litres water
1 large onion, peeled and quartered
3 carrots, peeled and quartered
3 celery stalks, with leaves if possible
a few black peppercorns

CHICKEN DUMPLINGS
2 chicken thighs
½ tsp freshly grated nutmeg
1 small garlic clove, peeled and crushed
2 tbsp very finely chopped fresh
    flat-leaf parsley
1 tbsp fresh breadcrumbs
1 medium egg
30g Parmesan, freshly grated

To make the stock, put all the ingredients into a large pan and bring to the boil. Gently skim off the scum as it rises to the surface using a large flat spoon. Reduce the heat, cover the pan with the lid and leave to simmer for at least 2 hours. Remove the chicken (use in a salad). Strain the stock and discard everything else. Once the stock has gone cold, remove any solidified fat. Chill to use within a day or two, or freeze. Season to taste when ready to use.

Make the pasta as described on page 30, then roll out and cut into small ribbons. Cover until needed.

To start the dumplings, bring 600ml of the stock to the boil and cook the chicken thighs in it until tender, about 15 minutes. When cool enough to handle, remove the chicken from the stock, and discard the chicken skin and bones. Keep the stock aside, this will be the wonderful basis for the soup.

Put the chicken meat into a food processor together with the remaining ingredients for the dumplings. You should have a fine paste, which you can roll into small quenelles. Use 2 tsp to make them.

Bring the stock to the boil, and add the pasta and the dumplings, and cook for a few minutes, until both are ready. Divide between warmed bowls, scatter over the celery leaves, if using, and serve sprinkled with Parmesan.

Pasta e Fagioli
{Pasta and Bean Soup }

Every Italian region, sometimes even every town, has a *pasta e fagioli*, which is a charming and warming *cucina povera* dish. It can be very thick or more soupy, according to the area of its origin. For me, it is a benchmark in my restaurants: if a chef can't make it properly, then he is not a good or conscientious chef. This southern version of the classic dish is totally different from the northern, and would traditionally make use of the leftovers of many packets of different pasta shapes, called *munnezzaglia* (rubbish). Nowadays, commercial pasta companies provide ready-mixed pasta in bags to be bought for the occasion, known as *pasta mista*.

SERVES 4

300g dried cannellini beans, soaked overnight
5 tbsp olive oil
a few pieces of cured Italian ham (prosciutto)
    and, if you can find it, a piece on the bone,
    or a handful of lardons
2 garlic cloves, peeled and sliced
10 cherry tomatoes, halved
1 litre beef or chicken stock
    (see pages 47 or 55)
200g mixed short dried pasta
2 tbsp fresh basil leaves
salt and pepper, to taste
extra virgin olive oil, to finish
1 tsp chopped fresh chilli (if liked),
    to finish

Drain the beans, and cover with fresh water (do not add salt). Cook them for 1½ hours until soft. Drain and reduce half of them to a paste in a processor.

In a large saucepan, heat the olive oil gently, then add the pieces of ham and the bone (if lucky enough to find one), and fry for about 2–3 minutes, then add the garlic, and fry very briefly. Add the tomatoes and the stock and bring to the boil. Add both the whole and crushed beans and the pasta, and cook, stirring occasionally, until the pasta is soft, about 10 minutes. Add the basil and salt and pepper to taste.

Divide the soup between warmed bowls and serve with a little stream of extra virgin olive oil. I wouldn't add any cheese, but perhaps a little choppd chilli would be good.

ALTERNATIVES

For a more northern version of this classic pasta soup, replace the dried cannellini beans with borlotti beans and the mixed short dried pasta with broken pieces of dried tagliatelle, add a finely chopped onion to the oil with the ham and scatter over a little freshly grated Parmesan to finish.

Stracciatella con Farfalline

{ Egg Soup with Small Butterflies }

This is probably the simplest of all soups, very welcome as comfort food in the autumn and winter months. The butterfly pasta is short and purposely made for soups. In restaurants you may find the *stracciatella* without pasta. Either way it would be good for children.

SERVES 4

1.5 litres chicken or beef stock
    (see pages 55 or 47)
30g unsalted butter
150g dried farfalline pasta
4 medium eggs, beaten (choose those with
    good yellow yolks, to give colour)
2 tbsp finely chopped fresh flat-leaf parsley
80g Parmesan, freshly grated
salt and pepper, to taste
extra virgin olive oil, for drizzling

Bring the stock to the boil in a large saucepan, and melt in the butter. Add the pasta and cook in the stock until soft, about 8 minutes.

Mix the beaten eggs, parsley and 50g of the Parmesan, and season with salt and pepper to taste. Stir this egg mixture into the hot stock and pasta, and serve immediately, sprinkled with the remaining Parmesan and a drizzle of olive oil.

ALTERNATIVES

Instead of the farfalline, when cooking for children you could use alphabet pasta. An alternative soup would be *zuppa pavese*, where fried bread is put in the bottom of the bowl (instead of pasta), and an egg and stock poured on top.

Couscous alla Trapanese

{ Sicilian Couscous with Clams }

Sicily loves strong flavours, but this quite delicate dish is an exception. The use of couscous reminds us that the African countries are just across the water from Italy. Sicily was the only region in Italy to adopt Arab influences, probably because the Arabs ruled there for over 200 years. Couscous is very often served in Morocco and other northern African countries with a fish sauce.

SERVES 4

6 tbsp olive oil
1 garlic clove, peeled and finely chopped
½ tsp chopped fresh chilli, to taste
750g small clams (*vongole*), cleaned
50ml dry white wine
150g quick-cook couscous
300ml fish stock (see below)
salt and pepper, to taste
1 tbsp finely chopped fresh flat-leaf parsley

FISH STOCK (MAKES ABOUT 2.25 LITRES)
1.2kg mixed white fish pieces
    (heads, bones, etc.)
4 litres water
a pinch of coarse sea salt
2–3 celery stalks, roughly chopped
2 carrots, peeled and cut into pieces
a bunch of fresh flat-leaf parsley
1 onion, peeled and halved
2 garlic cloves, unpeeled
1 tsp fennel seeds

To make the stock, wash all the fish pieces and bones under cold running water, then place in a saucepan with the water and a little salt. Bring to the boil and skim away the froth. Add all the remaining ingredients, cover with the lid and leave to simmer for an hour. Strain the liquid through a sieve, discarding everything else. Allow to cool. Keep for a couple of days in the refrigerator, or freeze. Season to taste before use.

Put the oil in a large saucepan, and fry the garlic and chilli very briefly. Add the clams and put the lid on. Agitate the pan a bit until the clams open, about 4–5 minutes. Add the wine, and cook for a minute to evaporate the alcohol.

Meanwhile, cook the couscous separately in 300ml of the stock, which will take about 4–5 minutes (see packet for instructions). It should still have some liquid in it.

Mix the two pans together, and serve, after tasting for seasoning. Sprinkle the brothy dishes with parsley. No Parmesan here.

Fregola Sarda in Brodo
{ Sardinian Pasta in Soup }

SERVES 4

1 litre chicken or beef stock (see pages 55 or 47)
150g dried fregola pasta
30g unsalted butter
50g pecorino cheese, freshly grated
2 tbsp chopped fresh chives
a few saffron threads (optional)
salt and pepper, to taste

Bring the stock to the boil in a large saucepan. Add the fregola, and cook for 12 minutes. Add the butter, the pecorino, the chives and a few saffron threads, if you like. Season to taste with salt and pepper and serve hot.

ALTERNATIVE

If you didn't have any fregola, you could use couscous in this simple but very warming soup. Rub some couscous together in slightly dampened hands to make imitation balls of fregola before adding to the recipe as before.

Zuppa di Pasta e Cavolfiore
{ Pasta and Cauliflower Soup }

SERVES 4

250g fresh eggless pasta (see page 31)
2 garlic cloves, peeled and chopped
2 tbsp olive oil
1.5 litres water
400g small cauliflower florets
salt and pepper, to taste
2 tbsp chopped fresh basil leaves
50g Parmesan, freshly grated
extra virgin olive oil, to finish

Roll out the pasta by hand or machine to 2mm thick. Cut into short bent noodles, about 15cm in length and 3cm wide. Cover until ready to use.

Fry the garlic in the oil for a few minutes until softened, then add the water and cauliflower. Bring to the boil, then cover the pan with a lid and simmer until the cauliflower is very soft, about 20 minutes. Now add the pasta and some salt and pepper to taste, and cook until everything is soft, about 5–6 minutes. Scatter over the basil and Parmesan and drizzle over a little stream of olive oil on top of each portion. Serve hot.

ALTERNATIVE

My mother used to cook this fresh pasta soup when there was not very much food around, although the topping of basil, Parmesan and oil is a new invention which adds a lot of extra flavour. Romanesco, that perfectly formed lime-green head of vegetable, halfway between cauliflower and broccoli, was not available when my mother was cooking, but could be used instead of the cauliflower.

Ciceri e Tria

{ Chickpea and Pasta Soup }

This is an old Roman recipe, at least 2,000 years old, but it is still delicious and appealing. It is usually found nowadays in Puglia. They often use lagane, which is a freshly made flour and water pasta (no egg).

SERVES 4

200g dried chickpeas, soaked for 24 hours
300g fresh eggless pasta (see page 31)
1 garlic clove, peeled and finely chopped
½ tsp fresh chopped chilli, to taste
4 tbsp olive oil
5 cherry tomatoes, quartered
2 tbsp fresh basil leaves
1.5 litres water
salt and pepper, to taste
extra virgin olive oil, to finish

Drain the chickpeas, and cover with fresh water (do not add salt). Cook them for $1\frac{1}{2}$ hours until soft. Drain and reduce about a third of them to a paste in a processor. Keep to one side.

Meanwhile, roll the pasta out by hand or machine to 2mm thick, and cut into medium ribbons, 5mm wide, about 20–25cm in length. Cover until ready to use.

In a large saucepan, fry the garlic and chilli in the oil for a few minutes, then add the tomatoes, both the whole and squashed chickpeas, the basil and water. Stir and then add the pasta. Cook gently for 5–6 minutes until tender. Taste for salt and pepper. Serve the soup hot, with a little stream of good extra virgin olive oil on top of each portion.

Minestrone di Verdure

{ Vegetable and Pasta Soup }

This version of *minestrone* is influenced by those served in Lombardy and Liguria, but you will find similar soups – and some surprisingly different kinds – throughout the country. Most *minestroni* use bits and pieces of vegetables left in the fridge, such as courgette, aubergine, carrot, celery, cabbage, quartered Brussels sprouts, etc. You could add some potatoes as well, to add thickness.

SERVES 4

4 tbsp olive oil
1 garlic clove, peeled and finely chopped
1 onion, peeled and finely chopped
2 litres chicken or beef stock
   (see pages 55 or 47)
about 1kg vegetables (see above), prepared
   and cubed
150g dried tubettini pasta
1 x 400g can borlotti beans, drained
3 tbsp fresh pesto (see page 69)
salt and pepper, to taste
40g Parmesan, freshly grated

Put the oil in a pan and fry the garlic and onion for a few minutes. Add the stock and prepared vegetables, and cook for about 12 minutes. Add the pasta and drained beans, and cook until tender, about another 6–7 minutes, then remove from the heat.

Mix in the pesto and salt and pepper to taste, and heat very gently. Serve straightaway, sprinkled with Parmesan.

ALTERNATIVES

If you don't want to have a vegetarian soup, you could add some Parma ham, prosciutto, cooked ham or bacon chunks. You could also use rice instead of pasta, or any other shape of pasta.

PASTA ASCIUTTA

PASTA WITH SAUCES

When you see *pasta asciutta* on Italian menus, it means pasta with a sauce as opposed to a pasta that is cooked in a soup or broth. *Asciutta* actually means dry, but this pasta is not completely dry: there should always be enough sauce to coat every pasta string or shape, but not so much that there is a sea of sauce swimming at the bottom of the plate when the pasta is eaten. In other words, you should be able to taste the pasta flavoured with a bit of sauce rather than just taste the sauce. Other nations may love to see a mass of sauce, bolognese or whatever, but this is not the Italian way.

Pasta asciutta also means a pasta that has to be eaten with a fork, which echoes the 'dry' characteristic above: if the dish is so soupy that a spoon is needed, then it is not properly *pasta asciutta*. Spoons in Italian pasta-eating are only used for soups and desserts, and are never used in conjunction with a fork when eating long pasta. (And it is absolutely forbidden to cut long pasta with a knife. The pasta is long and stringy for a purpose, to be twirled on a fork, without a spoon or a knife, to make a lovely mouthful.)

Pasta asciutta is usually *pasta corta*, the short shapes such as penne and fusilli – and indeed other flour and water products such as gnocchi – but it can also be *pasta lunga*, the long shapes such as spaghetti. *Pasta asciutta* can be flavoured with any kind of sauce, starting with the simplest tomato, but can also be based on other vegetables. The sauces can be of meat or game, or of fish, and I have divided the following chapter into three parts – vegetable, meat and fish – to make it easy for you to choose. All but the fish pasta dishes can be sprinkled with cheese, which will add savoury notes and its own inimitable flavour. The Italians tend to avoid using cheese with fish dishes because they think it drowns out the subtle flavour of the fish.

Spaghettini con Salsa Napoletana

{ Thin Spaghetti with Tomato Sauce }

This is one of my favourite sauces, because it is so simple, and I would choose it as my last meal. Naples is famous for its tomatoes, and it is here, more or less, that the tomato sauce for pasta was invented. In Naples they would make the sauce either with or without garlic, and with fresh ripe tomatoes. Elsewhere, when the tomatoes are not so ripe, Italians use very good chopped canned tomatoes.

SERVES 4

350g dried spaghettini pasta
salt and pepper, to taste

TOMATO SAUCE
5 tbsp olive oil
1 onion, peeled and finely chopped, or 2 garlic
    cloves, finely chopped, or both
600g ripe tomatoes, straight from the plant, or
    600g chopped or crushed canned tomatoes
about 2 tbsp fresh basil leaves, plus extra
    for garnish

Heat the oil in a large pan, and fry the onion or garlic (or both) for a few minutes. Add the tomatoes. Cook for a few minutes, no more than 10, and the sauce is ready. Add the basil and mix in.

Cook the pasta in plenty of boiling salted water for about 6–7 minutes or until *al dente*. Lift out with pasta tongs and put into the sauce. Mix well, season to taste and distribute equally with the amount of sauce between warmed plates. I don't usually put Parmesan on this one, but you can. Garnish with a few extra basil leaves if you like.

ALTERNATIVES

You can use many shapes of pasta with tomato sauce, *corta* and *lunga*. This is also an ideal sauce for those who have to eat gluten-free pasta.

Capelli d'Angelo alla Salsa di Tartufo
{ Angel's Hair Pasta with Truffle Sauce }

SERVES 4

300g dried capelli d'angelo pasta
salt and pepper, to taste
60g Parmesan, freshly grated

TRUFFLE SAUCE
80g unsalted butter, roughly chopped
1 tsp truffle oil
a few shavings of black truffle (optional)

Cook the pasta in plenty of boiling salted water, stirring well at the start to break up the little pasta nests, for 5–6 minutes or until *al dente*.

Meanwhile, for the sauce, put the butter in a pan and melt it. Add a tsp truffle oil. Stir well, then add about 3 tbsp cooking water from the pasta, to give a bit of additional moisture.

Lift the pasta from the water with pasta tongs, add it to the butter, season with salt and pepper and most of the Parmesan. Mix well, adding the truffle shavings if liked, and serve sprinkled with the remaining Parmesan.

Trenette al Pesto di Ponente
{ Trenette with West Ligurian Basil Sauce }

SERVES 4

150g waxy potatoes, diced
150g topped and tailed French beans
salt and pepper, to taste
400g dried trenette pasta
    (a flat spaghetti, similar to linguine)
60g Parmesan, freshly grated

PESTO
80g fresh basil leaves, without stalks
50g pine kernels
3 garlic cloves, peeled and coarsely chopped
a pinch of coarse sea salt
abundant olive oil, at least 120ml, or as required
50g Parmesan, freshly grated

For the pesto, mix the basil leaves, pine kernels, garlic and salt together in a mortar, and grind together with the pestle until you have a smooth paste. Add the olive oil and Parmesan and possibly 2 tbsp of the pasta cooking water if the mixture looks too dry. You want a semi-liquid texture.

Meanwhile, cook the potatoes and beans in a large pan of boiling salted water for 10 minutes, then add the trenette and cook for a further 10 minutes until the pasta is *al dente* and the vegetables are tender. Drain well, but save a little of the pasta water in case it is needed in the pesto.

Warm the pesto through very gently – you don't want to cook it – then add the pasta and vegetables. Mix well, season to taste and serve, sprinkled with grated Parmesan.

ALTERNATIVE
To vary this classic west Genoan version of the Ligurian basil sauce, known as pesto, try doing as they do in the eastern part of Genoa, mixing in some homemade junket, or crème fraîche, to make it paler and creamier.

Pennoni con Salsa di Sedano Rapa

{ Large Penne Pasta with Celeriac Sauce }

This is a new recipe. I have used celeriac, which I like very much, reduced to a pulp to form the basis of the sauce. The addition of ham in small strips (or smoked ham) lifts the sauce and makes it very appetising, though for a vegetarian version this can simply be omitted.

·

SERVES 4

300g dried large penne, pennoni, with ridges (rigate)
60g Parmesan, freshly grated
2 tbsp finely chopped fresh flat-leaf parsley
salt and pepper, to taste

SAUCE
50g unsalted butter
1 onion, peeled and finely chopped
100g cooked ham, cut into matchstick strips
600g celeriac, peeled and cut into small cubes
about 50ml milk

Melt the butter in a large saucepan and fry the onion for 5 minutes. Add the ham, and warm through. Set aside.

In a separate pan, cook the celeriac cubes in boiling salted water until very soft, about 10 minutes. Drain and add to the pan with the buttery onion. Squash it down a bit. Add the milk to make it more liquid, and warm through gently.

Cook the pennoni in plenty of boiling salted water for 8–10 minutes or until *al dente*. Drain and mix with the sauce in the pan. Sprinkle with the Parmesan and parsley, and lots of black pepper.

ALTERNATIVES

You could use macaroni, sedani, elbows or rigatoni.

Bucatini con Salsa di Peperoni Arrostiti e Acciughe

{ Large Spaghetti with a Roast Pepper and Anchovy Sauce }

Peppers, when roasted on charcoal, have a fantastic flavour, not of pepper at all. The combination with anchovy is delicious, and anchovies have been used since Roman times for flavouring many dishes. They have to be fillets in oil for this sauce, which reminds me of *bagna càuda*, an anchovy mixture we use as a dip in Piedmont. It is ideal for bucatini, large spaghetti with a hole: the hole, although too small for the sauce to penetrate, somehow makes the pasta lighter, adding another dimension to the dish.

SERVES 4

350g dried bucatini pasta
salt and pepper, to taste
2 tbsp finely chopped fresh flat-leaf parsley

SAUCE
2 large yellow and 2 large red peppers
6 tbsp olive oil
1 onion, peeled and finely chopped
10 anchovy fillets in oil

PASTA ASCIUTTA

Have your barbecue ready, and cook the peppers whole until the skin is charred. The steam inside will cook the flesh as well. Or hold the peppers over a gas flame – but the flavour won't be the same. Cool, then remove the skins. Cut the peppers in half, and remove the seeds and pith. Cut the flesh into little strips.

Meanwhile, heat half the oil in a pan and fry the onion until soft, about 6 minutes. Put half of the red pepper and yellow pepper strips into a blender with the remaining oil, the onion and its oil, and the anchovies, and blend. Return to the frying pan.

Meanwhile, cook the pasta in plenty of boiling salted water for about 8 minutes or until *al dente*. Drain and put it into the sauce in the pan, season to taste. Mix and divide between warmed plates. Decorate with the remaining pepper strips and some parsley.

ALTERNATIVES

You could use ciriole or fusilli instead of the bucatini.

Trofie con Salsa di Erbe e Noci

{ Pasta Twists with a Herb and Nut Sauce }

Trofie, little twists of pasta, mini fusilli, are Ligurian, and you won't find them anywhere else. Liguria is the region in the north where many herbs, notably basil, are used together with walnuts to make a lovely sauce. On the hills rearing up from the sea they grow various greens and herbs which are more perfumed, intense and delicious than anywhere else: perhaps the sea and its winds are influential. Another Ligurian classic, for example, is a stuffed pasta called pansòti, little tummies filled with those greens and served with a walnut sauce.

SERVES 4

300g dried trofie pasta
    (but best homemade, see page 37)
salt and pepper, to taste

SAUCE
150g shelled walnuts, last season's
½ tbsp each of chopped fresh oregano,
    rosemary and sage
a few basil leaves, sliced
10g coarse sea salt
2 garlic cloves, peeled
about 6 tbsp olive oil
80g pecorino cheese, freshly grated

Cook the trofie in plenty of boiling salted water for about 12–14 minutes (a long time, I know) or until *al dente*. (Fresh will take much less, about 4–5 minutes.)

Meanwhile, to make the sauce, in a pestle and mortar, crush the walnuts with the herbs, salt and garlic to obtain a creamy texture. Add the oil, and 60g of the pecorino, and make a lovely mixture.

Drain the trofie, saving a couple of tbsp of the cooking water, and put them in the sauce. The sauce just needs heating up, not cooking, with the addition of the saved pasta cooking water. Sprinkle with the remaining pecorino and any remaining basil leaves.

ALTERNATIVES

You could use trenette, which are similar to linguine, instead of the trofie. You could use toasted hazelnuts instead of the walnuts.

Cappelli con Caponata

{ Large Pasta Hats with Sicilian Vegetable Stew }

Cappelli, a traditional Puglian pasta that resembles little hats, is made from durum wheat semolina in Puglia. I have had the audacity to combine them with a typical Sicilian speciality, *caponata*, creating an Italian fusion dish, which I must confess is rather successful. It could be eaten warm or cold as a salad.

SERVES 4

350g dried cappelli pasta
salt and pepper, to taste

CAPONATA
2 large aubergines, cut into slices first
     and then cubes
100ml olive oil
2 onions, peeled and finely sliced
the heart of 1 head celery, plus the leaves,
     finely chopped
150g pitted green olives, sliced
200g tomatoes, ripe from the plant, crushed
50g salted capers, rinsed
2 tbsp caster sugar
2 tbsp strong red wine vinegar
10 fresh basil leaves, plus extra to garnish

Start by soaking the aubergine cubes in water to make them less oil-absorbent, for up to 10 minutes. Drain them well. Heat the oil in a large frying pan, then fry the aubergine until soft, about 10 minutes. Drain on absorbent kitchen paper and set aside.

In the same oil, fry the onions for a few minutes to soften, then add the celery, celery leaves, olives, tomatoes and capers, and cook until the celery is tender, about 10 minutes. Add the aubergine to the pan and stir-fry for a further 10 minutes. Add the sugar and the vinegar and cook for 5 minutes more. Add most of the basil and taste for salt and pepper.

Meanwhile, cook the pasta in plenty of boiling salted water for 12–14 minutes or until *al dente*. Drain and mix with the *caponata*. Add a drizzle of extra virgin olive oil, garnish with the rest of the basil leaves and serve.

Mafalde con Broccolo Romanesco e Acciughe

{ Pasta Ribbons with Romanesco and Anchovy Sauce }

Mafalde is a ribbon-type noodle, about 3cm wide, with one or both sides ruffled in order to catch sauces. Romanesco is of the cauliflower family, but is totally green, looking like a cross between cauliflower and broccoli, and tasting vaguely like cauliflower. The Romans used anchovies in almost everything, particularly a *garum* sauce, based on fermented fish, probably anchovies.

SERVES 4

PASTA ASCIUTTA

350g dried mafalde pasta
60g pecorino, freshly grated
salt and pepper, to taste

SAUCE
800g romanesco, cut into small florets
6 tbsp olive oil
3 garlic cloves, peeled and chopped
1 tsp chopped fresh hot red chilli
10 anchovy fillets in oil
finely grated rind of 1 lemon

ALTERNATIVES

Pappardelle or large tagliatelle could be used instead of the mafalde.

Cook the romanesco first in boiling salted water, for about 6–8 minutes or until soft. Drain.

Cook the pasta in plenty of boiling salted water for 12 minutes or until *al dente*. Drain, saving some of the cooking water.

In a large saucepan, fry in the oil the garlic and chilli, and when softened and still pale, about 4 minutes, add the anchovies and lemon rind and a couple of tbsp of the pasta cooking water. Add the romanesco, squashing some of the bigger florets. The texture of the sauce should be semi-liquid, so you will probably have to add some more water. Add pepper, but be careful of salt because the anchovies are already very salty.

Mix the pasta well into the sauce, and serve hot, sprinkled with the pecorino cheese.

Pasta Integrale con Salsa di Vegetali

{ Wholemeal Pasta with Vegetable Sauce }

SERVES 4

300g dried wholemeal spaghetti
salt and pepper, to taste
about 2 tbsp fresh basil leaves, torn
60g Parmesan, freshly grated

SAUCE
6 tbsp olive oil
2 onions, peeled and sliced
4 garlic cloves, peeled and chopped
2 medium carrots, peeled and very finely chopped
3 celery stalks, very finely chopped
4 medium tomatoes, finely chopped

For the sauce, heat the oil in a large saucepan and fry all the vegetables until soft, about 10 minutes.

Cook the spaghetti in plenty of boiling salted water for about 8–10 minutes (follow the instructions on the packet), or until *al dente*. Drain, save some of the cooking water, and mix the spaghetti with the sauce and taste for salt and pepper. Add the basil leaves and a little of the cooking water if required. Serve hot, sprinkled with the Parmesan.

Tortiglioni con Cipolla, Acciughe e Peperoncino

{ Spiral Pasta with Onion, Anchovy and Chilli }

SERVES 4

300g dried tortiglioni pasta
salt and pepper, to taste
50g aged Caciocavallo cheese, freshly grated

SAUCE
6 tbsp olive oil
1 onion, peeled and finely sliced
1 fresh hot red chilli, chopped
10 anchovy fillets in oil

Heat the oil in a large saucepan and fry the onion and chilli gently until very soft and still pale, about 10–12 minutes. Add at the end 2 tbsp water and the anchovies. They will dissolve quickly as you stir.

Cook the tortiglione in plenty of boiling salted water for 8–9 minutes or until *al dente*. Drain, mix with the sauce, season and serve hot, sprinkled with the grated cheese.

ALTERNATIVES

This sauce, which uses strong, traditionally Calabrian and Sicillian flavours, is excellent accompanied by gluten-free penne. It is also good with spaghettoni.

Gnocchetti Sardi con Carciofi e Topinambur

{ Sardinian Pasta with Globe and Jerusalem Artichokes }

Although I am using Sardinian pasta, this sauce is inter-regional, made all over the country when the uniquely small fresh globe artichokes are in season, in late winter/early spring. The Jerusalem artichoke is ready in autumn, but keeps well through the winter as it is a root vegetable. Globe artichokes are enjoyed all over Italy, but especially in Tuscany, Lazio and the entire south, including Sardinia. Jerusalem artichokes are quite often used as a dipping vegetable in Piedmont to accompany *bagna càuda*, the famous anchovy and garlic dip. (See recipe picture on page 83.)

SERVES 4

400g dried gnocchetti sardi
or malloreddus pasta
salt and pepper, to taste
a few saffron threads, toasted on a spoon over
a flame until dry, brittle and crushable, or a
sachet of powdered saffron
60g aged Parmesan or pecorino cheese,
freshly grated

SAUCE
8 very small fresh Italian globe artichokes
juice of 1 lemon
300g Jerusalem artichokes
5 tbsp olive oil
1 small onion, peeled and very finely sliced
100g frozen green peas
3 tbsp fresh flat-leaf parsley, finely chopped
100ml white wine

ALTERNATIVES

I usually serve this sauce with gnocchetti sardi,
but it would be also good with fresh or dried
egg tagliatelle, maltagliati, orecchiette
or pappardelle.

Clean the globe artichokes with a sharp knife so that you end up with the heart and the tenderest leaves. Cut the top of the artichokes, and peel down and remove most of the leaves until you reach the heart. Cut the heart in half, and scrape out any choke with a knife or spoon. Slice the halves thinly and put into a bowl of water acidulated with lemon juice to avoid oxidation. Peel the Jerusalem artichokes, and cut the flesh into small cubes. Add to the bowl.

To start the sauce, heat the oil in a large saucepan, and fry the onion for a few minutes until soft. Drain both types of artichoke, add to the pan and cook until the Jerusalem artichokes are soft and a little creamy, about 8 minutes. Add the peas and the parsley, along with the wine and about 50–100ml water, enough to make the sauce homogeneous. Take care that the sauce remains soft and not too thick.

Meanwhile, cook the pasta in plenty of boiling salted water for about 10–12 minutes or until *al dente*, and drain, leaving a little water in the pan. Add the saffron to this water, and mix with the pasta, which will become yellow. Add the pasta and saffron water to the sauce in the saucepan, season to taste and mix well. Serve in bowls, or on a sharing platter if you wish, with grated cheese sprinkled on the top.

Pennette Cacio e Pepe
{ Small Pasta Quills with Cheese and Pepper }

SERVES 4

350g dried pennette pasta
salt and freshly ground coarse black pepper, to taste
100g Parmesan or pecorino cheese, freshly grated

SAUCE
100g Parmesan, freshly grated
200g ricotta cheese
6 tbsp olive oil

Cook the pasta in plenty of salted boiling water for 6–8 minutes or until *al dente*. Drain, saving some of cooking water.

Mix the two cheeses and the oil into the drained pasta, stirring very well, adding a little of the pasta cooking water at the end. Grind in lots of black pepper, and serve, sprinkled with more Parmesan.

ALTERNATIVE

This dish, which is common to the whole of Lazio, can be made with other types of pasta, not just penne or pennette. The last time I had it was during the filming of a gargantuan pasta-eating competition while filming the second series of *Two Greedy Italians*. The proposition was that ten men would be able to eat a couple of kilos of pasta in one hour or more. I was the judge, and my eyes became bigger and bigger when I saw how much pasta those giants were shoving into their mouths!

Fusilli con Salsa alla Genovese
{ Spiral Pasta with a Genoese Onion and Tomato Sauce }

SERVES 4

500g dried fusilli pasta
salt and pepper, to taste
50g Parmesan, freshly grated (optional)
extra virgin olive oil

SAUCE
50ml olive oil
750g white onions, peeled and finely sliced
800g canned crushed tomatoes
1 tbsp tomato paste

Heat the oil in a large saucepan, and fry the onions very gently until they become transparent and soft, about 20 minutes. Add the tomatoes and tomato paste, salt and pepper to taste, and continue to cook on a low heat for 15 minutes.

Cook the pasta in plenty of boiling salted water for 8–9 minutes or until *al dente*. Drain well, then mix with the sauce and stir to coat all the pasta. Serve hot with optional Parmesan cheese and a little stream of extra virgin olive oil.

PASTA ASCIUTTA

Spaghetti Aglio, Olio e Peperoncino

{ Classic Spaghetti with Garlic, Olive Oil and Chilli }

This is the best-known gastronomical fast food, which can be enjoyed at any time of the day, even as a midnight feast, when you feel peckish. You can add an anchovy flavour if you like, using either anchovy fillets in oil or a salted anchovy sauce sold as *colatura* (and probably very similar to the Ancient Roman fish sauce, *garum*). Considered to be an aphrodisiac, this dish is known all over Italy.

SERVES 4

450g dried medium-sized spaghetti pasta
salt

SAUCE
60ml olive oil
6 garlic cloves, peeled and finely chopped
1 fresh hot red chilli, chopped
4 anchovy fillets in oil, or 1 tsp *colatura*
  (optional)

Cook the pasta in plenty of boiling salted water for 5–6 minutes or until *al dente*.

Meanwhile, heat the oil in a large saucepan and fry the garlic and chilli gently, without letting them brown. At this point you could add the anchovies and let them dissolve in the oil, or add the *colatura*. This sauce doesn't take more than 5 minutes to prepare.

Lift the cooked pasta from the water, using pasta tongs, and mix directly with the sauce. I wouldn't choose to use herbs or cheese here, but you can, only if you really insist.

Pennoni Giardiniera

{ Giant Quills with Courgette Sauce and Spinach Balls }

I have to include this recipe, because it has become very well known, at least in Carluccio's restaurants. Some years ago the personnel at the Ealing Carluccio's asked me if I could create a vegetarian dish with pasta. I went immediately to the kitchen, where I found enough courgettes and spinach to make a dish, matched them with pennoni (large pasta tubes from Puglia), and this is it. It has been on the Carluccio's menu since then, and each time it is ordered, it collects 50p for charity. It has been so successful that in those eight intervening years it has collected almost a million pounds!

SERVES 4

300g dried giant penne pasta, known as
    pennoni
salt and pepper, to taste
40g Parmesan cheese, freshly grated

SPINACH BALLS
600g young spinach leaves
2 medium eggs, beaten
1 garlic clove, peeled and crushed
tip of a knife of freshly grated nutmeg
50g fresh breadcrumbs
20g Parmesan, freshly grated
olive oil for shallow-frying

SAUCE
4 tbsp olive oil
1 garlic clove, peeled and finely chopped
1 little fresh red chilli, not too hot, finely
    chopped
300g grated courgette

Prepare the spinach balls first by cooking the spinach leaves in salted water for a few minutes. Scoop out and leave to cool down. When cool, squeeze out most of the moisture and chop the leaves with a knife, but not too small. Then mix in a bowl with the eggs, garlic, nutmeg, breadcrumbs and Parmesan. Make some balls the size of a large walnut and shallow-fry in oil until they start to brown on all sides. Set aside.

Cook the pasta in plenty of boiling salted water for 12–15 minutes or until *al dente*. Drain. (Pennoni are large, so need a longer cooking time.)

Meanwhile, for the sauce, heat the oil in a large saucepan, and add the garlic, chilli and courgette to the pan. Cook quickly in the oil, about 3–4 minutes. Add salt and pepper to taste.

Mix the cooked pasta into the sauce, then divide between warmed plates. Sprinkle the top of each portion with Parmesan and place four or five spinach balls on top.

ALTERNATIVES
You could use paccheri or rigatoni instead of the pennoni.

Maccheroncini con Frittedda

{ Macaroni with a Sauce of Asparagus, Onion, Peas and Broad Beans }

Frittedda is a speciality of Palermo, the capital of Sicily, where in springtime this young vegetable stew is eaten with *panelle*, chickpea flour fritters. I like it also as a sauce for pasta, and quite often add small, finely sliced artichoke hearts. This recipe is dedicated to Sicily, the first region in Italy to 'import' pasta – probably maccaruni – from the Arabs.

SERVES 4

350g dried maccheroncini pasta
50g Parmesan, freshly grated
salt and pepper, to taste

SAUCE
60ml extra virgin olive oil
2 onions, peeled and finely sliced
150g podded and peeled young broad beans,
    peeled weight
150g sweet young garden peas, podded
    weight
300g asparagus tips
2 tbsp finely chopped fresh flat-leaf parsley

Heat most of the oil in a large saucepan, add the onions and fry gently until soft, about 6–8 minutes. Add the raw broad beans, peas and lastly the asparagus tips. Add 100ml water and braise until the vegetables are tender, about 10 minutes. Add salt and pepper to taste.

Cook the pasta in plenty of boiling salted water for 6–7 minutes or until *al dente*. Drain well and mix with the sauce. Add the parsley and divide between four warmed plates. Sprinkle over the Parmesan and lastly pour on a stream of the remaining extra virgin olive oil. Serve hot.

ALTERNATIVES

This sauce is also good with egg tagliatelle or trenette.

Spaghettoni alla Carbonara

{ Classic Roman Pasta with Egg and Bacon }

The origins of this dish are various, some realistic, some fairly apocryphal! The use of the word *carbonara* suggests, however, that it is something to do with charcoal burners or coal porters – the black pepper representing flecks of coal. It could also have a hint of early 19th century politics, if associated with an undercover political movement called *Carbonari*, so called because they used to meet in cellars where the coal was kept. Either way, the recipe is definitely related to Rome and as such *guanciale*, preserved pork cheek, is used for the bacon. If you follow this recipe precisely, you might not end up with scrambled egg, which is usually the result! And you definitely don't use cream!

SERVES 4

500g dried spaghettoni pasta
salt and pepper, to taste

SAUCE
50ml olive oil
100g either smoked pancetta (bacon),
    guanciale or (as I tried and succeeded) fatty
    Parma ham, all cut into small cubes
3 medium whole eggs and 3 medium egg
    yolks, beaten
60g Parmesan or pecorino cheese,
    freshly grated
salt and pepper, to taste

Put the oil in a large saucepan and fry the cubes of whatever bacon or ham you use until crispy, about 5–6 minutes. Mix the beaten eggs with the cheese and lots of freshly ground black pepper.

Meanwhile, cook the pasta in plenty of boiling salted water for about 8 minutes or until *al dente*. Lift from the water with pasta tongs and put in a warm pan, off the heat, with the bacon and fat. The pasta shouldn't be too hot. Then pour in the egg mixture, and mix well so that the egg adheres to the pasta, just coating it, without curdling. Serve with more freshly ground black pepper.

ALTERNATIVES

Years ago Michael Palin gave me a can of Spam. On the back was written the recipe for Spam *carbonara*! I find this very funny, but I have never tried it. However, I have tried the recipe with black pudding, calling it Scottish *carbonara*. I substituted the *guanciale* with little cubes of a special black pudding from Stornoway, which was delicious. So you have the choice...

Penne all'Arrabbiata Calabrese

{ Pasta Quills with a Calabrian Style Chilli Sauce }

There are two regions in Italy which are very fond of chilli, and use it with abundance in their dishes, Abruzzi and Calabria. *Penne all'arrabbiata* is known all over the world, although it is sometimes wrongly served with the addition of cream! The sauce is usually made with garlic, tomatoes and chillies, but the Calabresi use *'nduja*, a really hot pork spreadable preserve, which looks like a large salami. The content is pork fat, usually from the loin or head (apart from the cheek, reserved for *guanciale*) and roasted hot red chilli pepper. The Calabresi spread *'nduja* on everything, and add it to many meat and pasta sauces. The idea and the name loosely derive from the French *andouille*, introduced in Angevin times, in the 12th century. The word *arrabbiata* means 'angry', and if you want the sauce hotter, you make it *incazzate* (which means 'very hot' or 'very angry')!

SERVES 4

400g dried penne rigate pasta
salt and pepper, to taste
80g pecorino or Caciocavallo cheese, freshly
    grated (optional)

SAUCE
50ml olive oil
3 garlic cloves, peeled and finely sliced
60g *'nduja* (available from a good Italian deli),
    or crushed chilli mixed with lard and tomato
    paste, to taste
400g canned crushed tomatoes

Heat the oil in a large pan and add all the garlic and *'nduja*. Fry briefly, then add the tomatoes and cook until the tomatoes reduce a little, leaving a wonderful sauce, about 10 minutes.

Cook the pasta in plenty of boiling salted water for 8 minutes or until *al dente*. Drain and add to the pan with the sauce. Mix well, distribute between warmed plates and if you want to add cheese sprinkle it on the top. I, however, prefer it without the cheese.

PASTA ASCIUTTA

ALTERNATIVES

This pasta dish is excellent with gluten-free penne. If you would like to use a different pasta shape then maccheroncini, small macaroni or, if you can't live without it, spaghetti are all good.

Mafalde al Ragù di Agnello

{ Pasta Ribbons with Lamb Sauce }

When I was filming in Basilicata a couple of years ago, I went into a trattoria, because of a wonderful smell: I discovered a lamb *ragù* steaming away in the kitchen. A plate of handmade strozzapreti pasta ('priest stranglers') and this lamb sauce was presented to me, and the taste is still strong in my memory. The priest stranglers are noodles, made from durum wheat semolina and water, which are slightly twisted on a thin rod such as a knitting needle. It is most unlikely that you will find these in a shop, which is why I have chosen the long pasta ribbons, which are curly on one or both sides, called mafalde. This recipe is associated with the south of Italy, with Basilicata and Puglia.

SERVES 4

500g dried mafalde pasta, or equivalent
60g pecorino or Parmesan cheese,
    freshly grated
salt and pepper, to taste

SAUCE
60ml olive oil
2 onions, peeled and finely sliced
1 small hot red chilli, chopped
1 carrot, peeled and finely cubed
1 celery stalk, finely cubed
4 bay leaves
1 whole shoulder of lamb, cut into chunks
2 fennel pork sausages, cut into chunks
200ml strong red wine
1kg ripe, fresh tomatoes or the equivalent of
    canned crushed tomatoes
2 tbsp tomato paste

ALTERNATIVE

This recipe would also be good with fusilli or even paccheri instead. Fennel pork sausages are fantastic with this sauce and are available from most good delicatessens.

Heat the oil in a large saucepan and add the onions. Fry until soft, about 8 minutes. Add the chilli, carrot, celery and bay leaves and stir-fry for about 5 more minutes. Now add the lamb and the sausages, and fry, stirring from time to time, until the meat gets some colour, about 5 minutes. Add the red wine, bring to the boil and let the alcohol evaporate for about 2 minutes. Add the tomatoes and the tomato paste and a little water if necessary, then cover and leave to cook slowly for $1\frac{1}{2}$ hours, uncovered, stirring from time to time. Add salt and pepper to taste, cook for another 20 minutes, and the sauce is ready. Should you have too much liquid fat swimming on top, take a sheet or two of absorbent kitchen paper, lay flat on top of the fat for a few seconds then discard. That should get rid of a good amount of fat.

Cook the pasta in plenty of boiling salted water for 12 minutes or until *al dente*. Drain the pasta and toss in a little of the sauce. Divide between warmed plates, topping equally with a piece of lamb and a piece of sausage. Sprinkle with pecorino (or, if you prefer, Parmesan), and enjoy with a glass of Pugliese red wine.

Paccheri con Ragù alla Napoletana

{ Large Pasta Tubes with Neapolitan Beef Sauce }

Hardly a family Sunday passes in Campania without a Neapolitan *ragù* being cooked and eaten for lunch. Probably derived from the French *ragoût*, which is slightly different (more a stew than a sauce), the Neapolitans have made this majestic dish their own. It is not just a sauce for pasta, but an entire meal, and the Neapolitans are very fussy about the cut of beef chosen to make the *braciola* (a stuffed piece of beef similar to the beef olive). They use *scamone*, rump of beef.

SERVES 4

400g dried paccheri pasta
60g Parmesan, freshly grated
salt and pepper, to taste

BRACIOLE
4 large thin slices of rump beef
2 tbsp coarsely chopped fresh flat-leaf parsley
1 tbsp raisins
1 garlic clove, peeled and crushed
20g Parmesan, freshly grated
1 tbsp pine kernels

SAUCE
60ml olive oil
1 onion, peeled and finely sliced
50ml dry white wine
800g canned crushed tomatoes
2 tbsp tomato paste

For the *braciole*, lay the slices of beef flat on a board. In a bowl, mix the parsley, raisins, garlic, Parmesan, pine kernels and some salt and pepper. Divide into four portions and spread onto the beef slices. Roll these up and fix either with a wooden toothpick or bind with kitchen string.

For the sauce, put the oil in a pan and fry the onion until softened, about 4–5 minutes. Add the beef *braciole* and fry to brown on eachside. Add the wine and let the alcohol evaporate for a few minutes, then add the tomatoes and the tomato paste. Stir well and let the mixture cook slowly at first, covered with the lid until boiling, then reduce the heat to a minimum. Add a little water if necessary. Cook for 1½ hours, uncovered, until the *braciole* are very tender. Turn this occasionally, and stir the sauce. Add salt and pepper to taste.

Cook the pasta in plenty of boiling salted water for about 10 minutes or until *al dente*. Drain the pasta and mix with some of the sauce. Serve each portion of pasta with some of the sauce and some grated Parmesan, and then serve the *braciole* separately, either sliced or whole, as a second course. Sunday lunch is done!

ALTERNATIVES

You could use rigatoni, vermicelli, fusilli or maccheroni instead of the paccheri.

Ciriole con Ragù di Quaglie

{ Square Spaghetti with Quail Sauce }

This is perhaps the gentlest *ragù* of them all and also the shortest in cooking time due to the tenderness of the meat. Ciriole is an Umbrian/Tuscan pasta, which is available dried, made with egg, but also fresh. It is made on the *chitarra*, a tool made of many wires stretched on a wooden box resembling a guitar. The wires are positioned next to each other, the fresh pasta sheet is laid on the wires and by pressing with a rolling pin, the pasta is cut into long square strands, all at the same time. The square shape offers the palate a completely different eating sensation from other pasta.

SERVES 4

PASTA ASCIUTTA

400g ciriole pasta, fresh or dried
60g Parmesan, freshly grated
salt and pepper, to taste

SAUCE
60ml olive oil
4 large quails (or pigeons or other small birds),
    cleaned (keep the giblets)
4 medium shallots, peeled and very
    finely sliced
100ml dry white wine
400g cherry tomatoes, halved
2 tbsp tomato paste, diluted with a little water
a pinch of freshly grated nutmeg
2 tbsp finely chopped fresh flat-leaf parsley,
    plus extra for serving

ALTERNATIVES

You could use bigoli instead of the ciriole, and you could replace the quail with a pheasant, duck or any wild bird.

Heat the oil in a large saucepan, add the cleaned quails and their giblets, and brown all over. Add the shallots and fry them until tender, about 5 minutes. Add the wine and let the alcohol evaporate for 2 minutes, stirring while cooking. Add the cherry tomatoes and the diluted tomato paste. Cook uncovered on a medium heat for 35 minutes until the tomatoes start to dissolve, stirring occasionally. Add the nutmeg. Remove the birds and bone them completely, returning the chopped meat and giblets to the sauce. Add the parsley and taste for salt and pepper.

Cook the pasta in plenty of boiling salted water for 8–10 minutes or until *al dente* if dried, and 4–5 minutes if fresh. Drain, mix with part of the sauce, then divide between warmed plates. Add more sauce and sprinkle with the grated Parmesan and a little extra chopped parsley.

Pinci con Ragù di Cinghiale

{ Fat Spaghetti with Wild Boar Sauce }

Italians like the taste of wild meat, and you might also encounter *ragùs* of venison, pheasant, hare and many other game animals and birds. The idea is always to cook the meat with some sauce very, very slowly, in order to extract all the flavours of the meat and vegetables. Pinci is a typically Umbrian pasta handmade from a dough of half Italian '00' flour and half durum wheat semolina flour and water. The strands look like shortish large spaghetti. They are about 20cm long, and pulled by hand. This recipe comes from Umbria/Tuscany.

SERVES 4

400g dried pinci pasta
salt and pepper, to taste
80g Parmesan, freshly grated

SAUCE
60ml olive oil
2 onions, peeled and finely sliced
1 carrot, peeled and finely cubed
1 celery stalk, finely cubed
600g wild boar meat, minced
50ml red wine
800g canned crushed tomatoes
1 tbsp tomato paste
1 tsp freshly grated nutmeg
6 bay leaves

Ragù always begins by heating the oil in a large saucepan, then adding and frying the onion, carrot and celery until softish, about 5 minutes. With this recipe, you then need to add the wild boar mince and brown it a little all over, stirring, before you add the wine. Stir for a few minutes to get rid of the alcohol. Add the crushed tomatoes and tomato paste, the nutmeg and bay leaves, and leave it to cook slowly, uncovered, for $1\frac{1}{2}$ hours, adding some water if necessary. Stir every now and then. Season with salt and pepper to taste when the sauce has reduced.

Cook the pasta in plenty of boiling salted water for 8–9 minutes or until *al dente*. Drain and mix with a little of the sauce. Plate the pasta with some more sauce on top and sprinkle with the grated Parmesan.

ALTERNATIVES

You can substitute the pinci with fusilli lunghi, paccheri, tripoline or pasta alla chitarra, a sort of square spaghetti. You could make a sauce like this in much the same way using rabbit, hare or venison meat.

Pappardelle con Ragù Soffritto

{ Pasta Ribbons with Lamb Offal }

This *soffritto* is for offal lovers, as it uses what the Italians call the 'fifth quarter' of the animal. My mother used to produce a lot of this, which was subsequently frozen and revived to use in soup: a small amount was added to some stock, the two were heated, then poured on a toasted slice of country bread in the bottom of the soup plate. Delicious. But I created this dish as a sauce for pasta, and all who have tasted it, said it is amazing. You have to order the offal, or pluck, at your butcher. This includes the entire interior of the lamb like the lungs, kidney, liver and heart. Discard the inedible parts like the trachea and some fat, and cut the rest into small cubes. This takes some time, but the taste of the finished dish is very rewarding.

SERVES 4

400g dried pappardelle pasta
salt and pepper, to taste
60g Parmesan, freshly grated (optional)

SAUCE
100g pure lard
60ml olive oil
4 garlic cloves, peeled and finely chopped
3 fresh hot red chillies, finely chopped
2kg lamb pluck (liver, lung, heart and kidney),
   very finely cubed
60ml red wine
400g canned crushed tomatoes
200g tomato paste
100ml beef or chicken stock
   (see pages 47 or 55)
10 fresh bay leaves

Heat the lard and oil together in a large saucepan, then add the garlic and chillies, and gently fry for a few minutes. Add all the lamb offal pieces, and stir-fry for 5 minutes. Add the wine and let the alcohol evaporate for 2 minutes. Add the crushed tomatoes and the tomato paste now, along with a little stock, and cook for 40 minutes with the bay leaves. Taste for salt and the sauce is ready.

Cook the pasta in plenty of boiling salted water for 5–6 minutes or until *al dente*. Drain and mix with some of the sauce to flavour and coat. Divide between warmed plates with more sauce in the centre, and add Parmesan if you want. Delicious!

Tripoline all'Amatriciana

{ Long Pasta with Tomatoes, Bacon, Olives and Pecorino }

SERVES 4

380g dried tripoline pasta
salt
60g aged and piquant pecorino cheese, freshly grated

SAUCE
60ml extra virgin olive oil
85g good *guanciale* (salted pig cheek) or *pancetta*,
  cut into small strips
1 small hot red chilli, whole (or chopped if you like it hot)
1 medium onion, peeled and very finely sliced
500g very ripe San Marzano or other plum tomatoes, cut
  through the length into 8 parts
10 black olives, pitted

Heat the oil in a large saucepan, and brown the *guanciale* briefly on a moderate heat. Add the chilli and onion and fry to soften, about 8 minutes. Add the tomatoes and olives, taste for salt and cook for 10 minutes.

Meanwhile, cook the pasta in plenty of boiling salted water for 7–9 minutes or until *al dente*. Drain and mix in the pan with the sauce. Sprinkle the individual portions with the cheese, and serve hot.

ALTERNATIVES

Instead of the tripoline, you could use bucatini, spaghetti or vermicelli for this much-loved dish from Rome.

Tagliatelle Fresche con Ragù alla Bolognese

{ Real Bolognese Sauce with Fresh Pasta Ribbons }

SERVES 4

450g fresh egg tagliatelle (see pages 29 and 33)
  or 400g dried egg tagliatelle
salt and pepper, to taste
100g Parmesan, freshly grated

SAUCE
80ml olive oil
1 large onion, peeled and finely chopped
500g lean minced pork
500g minced veal
150ml dry white wine
1kg canned crushed tomatoes or the same weight
  of freshly skinned and quartered tomatoes
4 tbsp tomato paste

Heat the oil in a large saucepan, add the onion and fry for a few minutes to soften and lightly brown it. Add the two meats and stir-fry for 6–8 minutes until brown. Add the wine and let the alcohol evaporate for 2 minutes. Add the tomatoes and the tomato paste. Stir and cook slowly, uncovered, for 1½ hours. Stir from time to time in case it sticks. Add salt and pepper to taste.

Cook the fresh pasta in plenty of boiling salted water for 4–5 minutes or until *al dente*. (Dried will take a little longer.) Drain and toss with some of the sauce to coat. Serve on hot plates with a further spoonful of the sauce and some grated Parmesan sprinkled on top.

ALTERNATIVE

You could add carrot and celery to the basic sauce, along with the onion, if you wanted. But whatever you do, do not put herbs or garlic in this sauce – it should be very simple and doesn't need any special seasoning, as the intensity of flavour should come from the meat.

Tagliolini al Limone con Gnocchi di Pollo

{ Lemon Pasta Ribbons with Chicken Dumplings }

This is a variation on my chicken broth with chicken dumplings. In Italian cuisine you can use all the ingredients in different ways, and this hybrid recipe is still very Italian, because of its simplicity, along with lots of flavour, that appeals to the appetites of the Italians. The idea comes from Piedmont in the north.

SERVES 4

250g tagliolini pasta, fresh if possible
salt and pepper, to taste
60g Parmesan, freshly grated

CHICKEN DUMPLINGS
350g chicken flesh, minced
2 medium eggs, beaten
2 tbsp fresh breadcrumbs
1 garlic clove, peeled and crushed
2 tbsp finely chopped fresh flat-leaf parsley
6 fresh basil leaves, torn
a little freshly grated nutmeg
60ml olive oil
finely grated rind of 1 lemon,
    and the juice of ½ lemon

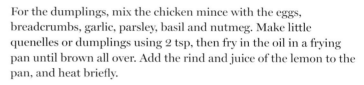

For the dumplings, mix the chicken mince with the eggs, breadcrumbs, garlic, parsley, basil and nutmeg. Make little quenelles or dumplings using 2 tsp, then fry in the oil in a frying pan until brown all over. Add the rind and juice of the lemon to the pan, and heat briefly.

Cook the pasta in plenty of boiling salted water for 5 minutes (if fresh) or until *al dente*. Drain, reserving a little of the pasta water, and toss together with the dumplings and their juices. Stir in the reserved pasta water, scatter over the Parmesan and serve.

ALTERNATIVES

Instead of tagliolini you can also use angel's hair (capelli d'angelo) or fettucce.

Spaghetti di Farro con Luganega

{ Spelt Spaghetti with Sausage Sauce }

Most commonly, an ancient wheat type called 'spelt' is called *farro* in Italy. In fact, a closely related rare wheat, in English 'emmer', is correctly the botanical equivalent of *farro*. (Like the history of pasta, the untangling of grain types is a minefield.) Spelt was used long before our modern-day wheat because it was easy to grow in almost every region of Italy. But it is in Tuscany and Umbria that it is still used today, in modest quantities, in the making of both bread and pasta (and risotto-type dishes). The flavour of both pasta and bread is different, with a wholemeal characteristic, which makes it less delicate and nuttier than ordinary wheat pasta. Combining spelt pasta with *luganega*, a tasty sausage originating from Greece, seems to be ideal.

SERVES 4

350g dried spelt spaghetti pasta
salt and pepper, to taste
60g pecorino cheese, freshly grated

SAUCE
30g dried *porcini,* rehydrated
3 tbsp olive oil
50g unsalted butter
1 small onion, peeled and finely chopped
½ fresh hot red chilli, finely chopped
250g sausage *(luganega)*, meat removed from the skin and crumbled
100ml white wine
2 tbsp tomato paste, diluted in 2 tbsp water
1 tbsp fresh rosemary needles

Soak the dried *porcini* for the sauce in hot water for 20 minutes, then drain, reserving the soaking water, and chop.

Heat the olive oil in a large saucepan with the butter, and fry the onion and chilli briefly. Add the crumbled sausage and *porcini*, and fry and stir for 8–10 minutes. Add the wine and then cook for a further 2 minutes until the alcohol has evaporated. Add the tomato and rosemary and cook for another 10 minutes on a low heat. Season with salt and pepper to taste, and if more moisture is needed, add some of the *porcini* soaking water.

Meanwhile, cook the pasta in plenty of boiling salted water for about 10–15 minutes or until *al dente* (follow the packet instructions). Drain well. Mix with the sauce and divide between deep warmed plates. Sprinkle with the cheese and eat straightaway.

ALTERNATIVES

Obviously the sauce would go with any spaghetti or other long pasta, or indeed with penne. If you leave the sausage in larger chunks, the sauce would be good served with polenta. *Luganega* sausages are available from good butchers or delicatessens.

Spaghettoni con Polpette di Carne e Melanzane

{ Large Spaghetti with Meat and Aubergine Balls }

It is well known that pasta is the best food for endurance athletes, especially before a physically engaging event such as a marathon. This is because pasta is very slowly digested, which allows energy to be released over some considerable time. I created this recipe especially for my rugby-playing friends, and it has worked well as demonstrated by Italy's recent win over France. (Rugby is a sport I would have enjoyed if, when I was young, I had been introduced to it.)

SERVES 6 GENEROUSLY

600g good-quality dried spaghettoni
30g Parmesan, freshly grated
salt and pepper, to taste

SAUCE
50ml olive oil
1 large onion, peeled and very finely chopped
100ml dry white wine
2 tbsp tomato paste
680g tomato passata
10 fresh basil leaves

MEATBALLS
2 whole aubergines
olive oil for cooking and shallow-frying
300g lean minced beef
1 garlic clove, peeled and squashed to a paste
½ tsp freshly grated nutmeg
50g Parmesan, freshly grated
1 medium egg, beaten
100g fresh breadcrumbs

SERVING SUGGESTION

An accompanying glass of *Barbaresco* or *Chianti Classico* – unless the players have to play soon afterwards – would suit this dish very well!

Preheat the oven to 180°C/Gas 4. Put the aubergines for the meatballs in an ovenproof dish, drizzle with a little olive oil and bake for 30 minutes. Cut the aubergines in half, and scoop the pulp out of the skins. Mash the pulp and keep to one side. Discard the skins.

For the sauce, heat the olive oil in a large saucepan, and fry the onion until soft, about 5 minutes. When soft add the wine, the tomato paste, tomato passata and the basil. Stir well and leave to cook gently for 30–40 minutes.

Meanwhile, continue with the meatballs by mixing together the beef mince, the soft aubergine pulp, garlic paste, nutmeg, Parmesan, beaten egg, breadcrumbs and some salt and pepper in a bowl. Mix well and shape with your hands into the shape of rugby balls and the size of apricots. Shallow-fry in olive oil to brown on all sides. Add the balls to the tomato sauce and keep warm.

Cook the pasta in plenty of boiling salted water for 8 minutes or until *al dente*. Drain well.

Pour the pasta into a large deep serving dish, and mix well with half of the sauce. Divide between individual dishes, put the rest of the sauce on the top and sprinkle with the Parmesan.

Lorighittas ai Frutti di Mare

{ Sardinian Spiral Ring Pasta with Seafood }

I came across this type of pasta in the Sardinian restaurant, Olivomare, in London. It is made by hand and looks like little circles of woven dough, which is very responsive to the eye and palate. You can find it dried in good Italian delicatessens. Which seafood you choose is up to you alone, but the items have to be very fresh.

SERVES 4

400g dried lorighittas pasta
salt and pepper, to taste
4–6 fresh basil leaves, to garnish

SAUCE
60ml olive oil
2 garlic cloves, peeled and finely chopped
10 cherry tomatoes, halved
40ml dry white wine
1kg seafood, cleaned weight, mixed, such as clams, mussels, scallops (with coral), prawns, baby octopus and baby squid (cut into rings)
10 fresh basil leaves

Heat the oil in a large saucepan, add the garlic and fry briefly before adding the cherry tomatoes. Add the white wine, and cook until the tomatoes are soft, about 10 minutes. Now add the cleaned clams and mussels. Cover with a lid and steam for 3–4 minutes. Add the other seafood and the basil, bring to the boil then simmer uncovered for 3–4 minutes.

Meanwhile, cook the pasta in plenty of boiling salted water for 10 minutes or until *al dente*. Drain, add to the sauce, mix well and serve with some fresh basil leaves and pepper on top.

ALTERNATIVES

You could use fusilli or any kind of spiral-shaped pasta instead of the lorighittas.

Farfalle con Grancevola e Gamberetti

{ Butterfly Pasta with Spider Crab and Small Prawns}

You need to work quite hard to obtain all the meat from a spider crab – ask your fishmonger to do this for you, he knows exactly what he is doing! The spider crab is at home in the Venetian Lagoon, but much bigger examples are found in the North Atlantic and the North Sea and can be found occasionally in good fishmongers. It has a very delicate flavour and texture, and to accompany pasta, I think it needs some additions, such as the prawns, herbs and spices.

SERVES 4

350g dried medium farfalle pasta
3 tbsp finely chopped dill or fresh
    flat-leaf parsley

SAUCE
250g ready prepared spider crab meat
150g small raw prawns
1 aubergine, peeled and cut in slices
salt and pepper, to taste
6 tbsp olive oil
1 garlic clove, peeled and finely chopped
150g leeks, finely chopped
1 tbsp fennel seeds
50ml white wine

ALTERNATIVES
You could vary the pasta, using long angel's hair or linguine instead of the chunkier farfalle. If you can't find spider crab, you can of course substitute with a commoner type of crab, which has both white meat and the more strongly flavoured brown meat.

Either get the fishmonger to take out the meat and remove the dead man's fingers from the freshly cooked spider crab, or buy the meat ready prepared (but check for freshness). Boil the small prawns in water for about 2–3 minutes, then drain and peel.

Cook the aubergine in slightly salted water until soft, about 5 minutes, then mash. Heat the oil in a large saucepan, and fry the garlic and leeks until soft: do not let them brown. Add the fennel seeds and the mashed aubergine, and fry for a minute or two before adding the wine and mixing well. Cook gently for a few minutes. Add the crab meat and the prawns, stir and heat through, and taste for salt and pepper.

Meanwhile, cook the pasta in plenty of boiling salted water for 8–9 minutes or until *al dente*. Drain well, and mix with the sauce. Serve sprinkled with the dill or parsley.

Tonnarelli con Seppioline e Gamberetti

{ Black Ink Pasta Ribbons with Baby Cuttlefish and Prawns }

Tonnarelli is a long pasta like tagliatelle, but it has a square profile (as if cut on a *chitarra* – see page 104). The strands are usually plain white but also come flavoured and coloured with squid ink. Buy them dried in good delicatessens, or have a go at making your own long black pasta using the cuttlefish ink available at good fishmongers' shops.

SERVES 4

400g dried black tonnarelli pasta or
    450g fresh long black pasta (see page 31)
salt and pepper, to taste
2 tbsp coarsely chopped fresh flat-leaf parsley

SAUCE
80ml olive oil
2 onions, peeled and finely sliced
30ml white wine
300g baby cuttlefish, cleaned of ink, chopped
200g small prawns, peeled

ALTERNATIVE

An obvious choice would be replacing the tonnarelli with black (or white) spaghetti.

Heat the oil in a large saucepan, and fry the onions until soft, about 8 minutes. Add the wine and let the alcohol evaporate for 2 minutes. Add the cuttlefish pieces along with the prawns and cook for 5–6 minutes. Season with salt and pepper to taste.

Meanwhile, cook the pasta in plenty of boiling salted water for 6 minutes or until *al dente*. Drain and mix with the sauce and the parsley. Serve hot.

Fettuccine Nere con Cipolle e Acciughe

{ Black Ink Pasta Ribbons with Onion and Anchovies }

SERVES 4

400g dried black fettuccine or spaghetti pasta
salt and pepper, to taste

SAUCE
80ml olive oil
500g onions, peeled and finely sliced
1 medium hot red chilli, chopped
10 good-quality anchovy fillets in oil

Heat the oil in a large saucepan and fry the onions and chilli for a few minutes, before adding about 50ml water to help them soften. When soft add the anchovy fillets and let them melt into the onions, stirring constantly.

Cook the pasta in plenty of boiling salted water for 6–7 minutes or until *al dente*. Drain, mix well with the sauce, season to taste and serve hot.

ALTERNATIVE

Venice is where the black ink of *seppioline* (cuttlefish) is most popular; and the city's black risottos and tagliatelle dishes are famous the world over. You can buy black pasta dried in good delicatessens, but if you can't find any then an obvious substitution is bigoli, which will turn this into the classic Venetian dish, *Bigoli in Salsa*.

Linguine con Salsa di Finocchio e Gamberi

{ Long Pasta with Fennel and Prawn Sauce }

SERVES 4

400g dried linguine pasta
salt and pepper, to taste
extra virgin olive oil, to finish

SAUCE
1kg young fennel bulbs
60ml olive oil
2 shallots, peeled and finely sliced
2 tbsp fresh dill tops, chopped
250g small raw peeled prawns

Wash and chop the fennel bulbs into smaller pieces. Heat the oil in a large saucepan and fry the shallots for 2–3 minutes. Add the fennel and enough water to almost cover. Fry/braise until the water has evaporated, about 8–10 minutes. Add the dill, some salt and plenty of pepper. Add the raw peeled prawns and cook for 5 minutes. The sauce is then ready.

Cook the pasta in plenty of boiling salted water for 7–8 minutes or until *al dente*. Drain well, toss with the sauce and serve hot, with a little stream of olive oil over the top of each bowl.

ALTERNATIVES

Linguine is the ideal pasta for a seafood sauce, and fennel is an ideal accompaniment for seafood, so it is hard to suggest an alternative to this recipe (which I am very happy with). If you do not have any linguine at home you could use capelli d'angelo, spaghetti or even tagliolini in its place.

Vermicelli e Gioielli di Mare in Cartoccio

{ Vermicelli and Sea 'Jewels' in a Bag }

I always wondered why some restaurants and *trattorie* served pasta with a mainly fish sauce in a bag made of ovenproof paper or aluminium foil. Through investigation I came to the conclusion that it is not only for show, but to properly cook and present the fish and pasta. It concentrates the flavour and fragrance, which explode when the package is opened, invading your nostrils with a truly pleasurable aroma. You must of course use the freshest of ingredients. If you can't get hold of a sea truffle – rare even in Italy – use some clams, they are all jewels of the sea. You will also need some good ovenproof paper or foil.

SERVES 4

PASTA ASCIUTTA

350g dried vermicelli or spaghetti pasta
salt and pepper, to taste

SAUCE
60ml olive oil
2 garlic cloves, peeled and finely sliced
1 hot red chilli, chopped
250g cherry tomatoes
2 tbsp dry white wine
300g mussels, cleaned
300g sea truffle or clams, cleaned
200g baby squid, cleaned, bodies cut
    into rings
200g very fresh prawns, peeled or unpeeled
200g scallops, cleaned and shelled weight
2 tbsp coarsely chopped fresh flat-leaf parsley

ALTERNATIVES

Linguine could be an alternative pasta, and you can use whatever seafood you can find or get hold of.

Preheat the oven to 200°C/Gas 6.

Heat the oil in a large saucepan, add the garlic and chilli, and fry briefly. Add the tomatoes and wine and cook for a few minutes. Now add the mussels and sea truffles or clams, put on the lid, and wait for them to open in the heat, about 4 minutes.

At this stage, cook the pasta in plenty of boiling salted water for 6–8 minutes or until *al dente*. While the pasta is boiling add the squid, prawns, scallops and parsley to the sauce, and cook for 3–4 minutes. Now add the well drained pasta to the sauce, mix well and season to taste.

To prepare the bag, lay a large doubled piece of paper or a single piece of foil out on a baking sheet on the work surface, roughly 50cm square. Put the pasta and sauce in the centre, and proceed to fold the parchment or foil in such a way as to to build a sealed dome. Seal all the edges well.

Put the baking sheet and the dome package into the hot oven for 5–6 minutes. Transfer the package to a large serving dish and bring to the table. Open in front of the guests and divide between warmed plates.

Trofie con Bottarga e Arselle

{ Pasta Twists with *Bottarga* and Clams }

Trofie is a short twisted pasta developed in Liguria: it is often handmade and cooked fresh, but it can be bought dried. *Arselle* or *vongole* are local clams, and the *bottarga*, the air-dried and salted roe of grey mullet (or tuna), is from Sardinia or Sicily and is available from most good delicatessens. It is good to mingle ingredients from different regions, the results will still be Italian! Trofie are usually eaten with pesto.

SERVES 4

400g dried trofie pasta
salt and pepper, to taste
80g grey mullet *bottarga*, freed from the
    protecting wax and very finely sliced

SAUCE
80ml extra virgin olive oil
1 small onion, peeled and finely sliced
1 garlic clove, peeled and pulped with a pinch
    of salt
10 cherry tomatoes, halved
1kg clams in the shell, cleaned
3 tbsp finely chopped fresh flat-leaf parsley

The pasta will take longer than the sauce, so start cooking it first. Cook the trofie in plenty of boiling salted water for about 12–14 minutes or until *al dente*. (Fresh will take much less time, about 4–5 minutes.)

Meanwhile, heat the oil in a large saucepan, add the onion and garlic and fry for 1 minute. Add the tomatoes and the clams, put the lid on and wait until they open, which will be minutes only. Remove briefly from the heat, and when cool enough, discard half of the clam shells, putting the meat back into the sauce. Cook the sauce for a few minutes until the tomatoes dissolve. Add the parsley, and some salt and pepper to taste.

Drain the pasta when ready, and add to the sauce. Divide between warmed plates, and scatter the *bottarga* slices over the top of each portion. Eat hot.

ALTERNATIVES

You could use garganelli, homemade or dried, or cecatelli instead of the trofie.

Capelli d'Angelo Neri con Due Bottarghe

{ Black Angel's Hair Pasta with Two Types of *Bottarga* }

Angel's hair is the thinnest kind of spaghetti, and it is available commercially in white or black, and dried; though you could make it fresh by following the master pasta-making recipe on page 29. The two types of *bottarga* used here are of grey mullet and tuna: the tuna can be grated, the mullet sliced. This gives an intense pleasant fishy flavour to the pasta, a little bit of a taste of the Mediterranean.

SERVES 4

350g dried black capelli d'angelo pasta
salt and pepper, to taste
100g tuna *bottarga*

SAUCE
50ml olive oil
2 garlic cloves, peeled and finely sliced
1 small hot red chilli, finely chopped
1 tbsp finely chopped chives
1 tbsp chilli oil *(see below)*
100g grey mullet *bottarga*, freed from the
   protecting wax and very finely sliced

Cook the pasta in plenty of boiling salted water for 2–4 minutes or until *al dente*.

Meanwhile, put the oil in a pan and fry the garlic, chilli and chives for a few minutes without browning.

When cooked, drain the pasta and mix with the sauce, the chilli oil and sliced mullet *bottarga*. Divide between warmed plates, and grate the tuna *bottarga* abundantly on top. Serve immediately.

MAKING CHILLI OIL

If you want to make chilli oil at home, put a couple of dried chillies – at least – into a bottle of ordinary olive oil (don't use the best extra virgin). Leave to infuse for a month. Never use fresh chillies, as they would go off.

Spaghettini ai Ricci di Mare e Patelle

{ Limpets and Sea Urchins with Thin Spaghetti }

I write this recipe in the knowledge that not everybody will be able to cook it because you need to be near the sea and in areas where these creatures are available. However, to me it is one of the most delightful seafood-eating experiences, and I have enjoyed it many times. Ask your trusted fishmonger, and he may be able to perform miracles, but don't be tempted to cook with any canned stuff. Limpets are those pyramidal shells attached to the rocks and available when the tide is low. The sea urchins have to be lifted from under the water as well: they too are attached to rocks but also cling to the bottom of a not-too-deep sea. You need quite a number of sea urchins because the edible coral-coloured 'roes' inside are not very big.

SERVES 4

400g dried spaghettini pasta
salt and pepper, to taste

SAUCE
roe of 40 sea urchins (yes!)
60ml olive oil
2 shallots, peeled and finely chopped
10 cherry tomatoes, halved
25 limpets (having removed the muscle off the bottom of the shell with a knife and cleaned)
1 tbsp finely chopped fresh chives

ALTERNATIVE
You could use linguine instead of spaghettini.

To prepare each sea urchin, wearing gloves, cut away around the mouth with a pair of heavy scissors or kitchen shears, and remove the top. Very carefully scrape away the five lines of roe, you don't want to puncture them. Get rid of the liquid and any black stuff. Set aside the roe.

Heat the oil in a large saucepan, and gently fry the shallots for 4–5 minutes. Add the tomatoes and let them soften for 10 minutes. Add the limpet meat and the chives, and cook gently for about 8 minutes.

Cook the pasta in plenty of boiling salted water for 6 minutes or until *al dente*. Drain, mix with the sauce and taste for salt and pepper. Serve with a quarter of the sea urchin roes on each plate. Mix and enjoy. The taste of the sea urchin will explode in your mouth!

Rigatoni e Scorfano

{ Scorpion Fish with Chunky Pasta }

There are two varieties of scorpion fish found in the Mediterranean, one black and quite small, the other red and up to 60cm in length. They are quite ugly fish (*scorfano* means 'ugly'), and on the dorsal fin there are some poisonous spines which you should try to avoid (ask the fishmonger to remove these, and to clean and gut the fish for you). But the meat is wonderful...

SERVES 4

400g dried rigatoni pasta
salt and pepper, to taste

SAUCE
60ml olive oil
2 garlic cloves, peeled and finely sliced
800g canned crushed tomatoes
either 8 small black scorpion fish, or 1 large
    red, about 1kg, cleaned and gutted
2 tbsp finely chopped fresh flat-leaf parsley
8 fresh basil leaves

ALTERNATIVES

Rigatoni can be replaced by mezze maniche, paccheri or other large short pasta shapes. If you can't find scorpion fish – and it could be difficult – you could use sea bream instead.

Heat the oil in a large saucepan, and fry the garlic gently for a few minutes, making sure not to brown it. Add the tomatoes and bring to the boil. Put the fish into the tomatoes and cook gently for 20–30 minutes, depending on the size of the fish.

Lift the fish onto a plate and take off all the meat. Be careful of the spikes, then discard all the bones. Return the meat to the sauce, heat up and add the parsley, the basil and salt and pepper to taste.

Meanwhile, cook the pasta in plenty of boiling salted water for 10–12 minutes or until *al dente*. Drain and mix with the sauce. Divide between warmed plates and eat immediately.

Sedani con Vodka e Salmone Affumicato

{ Large Pasta Tubes with Vodka and Smoked Salmon }

I don't want to admit to age, but my memory does go a long way back! Long enough to remember Giorgetto Giugiaro, one of the most famous Italian car designers (he designed the Fiat Uno and the DeLorean amongst many others), whom I met when I was filming for a BBC programme about Italy in the mid-1980s. For the pasta company Voiello, Giorgetto created a type of pasta on the drawing board specifically for collecting more sauce. This very stylish pasta was called marille, and it is a pity that Voiello has stopped producing it. This is the recipe Giorgetto cooked for me in his office. Sedani is a pasta that has similar characteristics to marille: it looks like a largish tube with ribbing on the outside.

SERVES 4

350g dried sedani pasta
salt and pepper, to taste

SAUCE
40ml olive oil
1 onion, peeled and finely sliced
750g canned crushed tomatoes
10 fresh basil leaves, plus extra to garnish
10ml vodka
50ml double cream
125g smoked salmon, cut into strips

ALTERNATIVES
You could use rigatoni or gomiti instead of the sedani.

Heat the oil in a large saucepan, and fry the onion until soft, about 5 minutes. Add the tomatoes, basil and vodka and cook for another 15–20 minutes.

Meanwhile, cook the pasta in plenty of boiling salted water for 10–12 minutes or until *al dente*. Drain. Add the cream to the sauce and mix well with the pasta. Divide between warmed plates, and serve with the salmon strips on top. Sprinkle with salt and pepper and garnish with a few torn basil leaves.

Linguine con Triglie al Curry

{ Linguine with Curried Red Mullet }

One of the most delicate fish, the red mullet has only one disadvantage, its bones. However, its rich-tasting flesh is worth it, I promise! The Italians have been exploring the new wave of spices, and several are now used in the first Italian attempts at 'fusion' cooking. (In fact the use of spices is a rediscovery because they were used in Italy in the Middle Ages.) One of their favourite spice mixtures is curry powder which, if used minimally and not generously as in the Indian way, adds a completely new dimension of flavouring.

SERVES 4

400g dried linguine pasta
salt and plenty of pepper, to taste

SAUCE
6 tbsp olive oil
2 fresh red mullet, about 500g each,
    scaled and gutted
3 garlic cloves, unpeeled
½ small hot red chilli, finely chopped
100ml white wine
680g good-quality tomato passata
1 tsp mild curry powder
2 bay leaves
2 tbsp finely chopped fresh flat-leaf parsley,
    plus extra to serve

Heat the oil in a frying pan, and add the fish, the unpeeled garlic and the chilli. Fry the fish gently for 10 minutes on each side, then add the wine and leave to cool down. Take the fish out of the pan and fillet them: discard the fish heads and all the bones and set the flesh aside. Add the tomato passata to the juices in the frying pan along with the curry powder and bay leaves. Simmer a little, about 10 minutes, then add the fish meat, the parsley and salt and pepper to taste.

Cook the pasta in plenty of boiling salted water for 7–8 minutes or until *al dente*. Drain well, add to the sauce, mix well and serve hot.

ALTERNATIVES

You could use spaghettini or tagliatelle instead of the linguine, and the red mullet could be replaced by cod or scallops.

PASTA FRESCA E RIPIENA

FRESH AND FILLED PASTA

The techniques needed to produce fresh stuffed or filled pasta are various; from using just your hands to taking advantage of little gadgets like the *raviolatrice*, a flat, aluminium grid with cavities for producing ravioli (see page 39). Whichever way you make it, the efforts involved in preparing filled pasta yourself really pay off.

One of the main joys of filled pasta is what you put inside. This concept is very close to the heart of every Italian cook, because on the whole these fillings utilise leftovers, minced with a bit of cheese perhaps and some breadcrumbs or egg to thicken. Because these pasta fillings contain various and very tasty ingredients already, the sauces which accompany filled pasta are kept very simple – often just a little butter and a sprinkling of cheese is used, or perhaps the deglazing juices of a pan in which meat has been roasted.

You can make fresh filled pasta a day ahead and store it in the fridge in a sealed container. I am a little wary about freezing filled pasta because you have to be sure that the filling will keep well, and that it cooks right through when you bring it out of the freezer. The alternative to eating your own fresh filled pasta is to buy from a local supplier, but this should only be considered if you really trust their quality. Although it is very quick and easy to use the semi-fresh vacuum-packed filled supermarket pastas, I really wouldn't recommend them because the taste of the filling is usually slightly artificial – and certainly nothing like as good as the pasta recipes in this chapter.

Tagliatelle di Castagne con Salsa di Funghi

{ Chestnut Tagliatelle with a Mushroom Sauce }

What a wonderful combination of two items from the woods, both of which are in season in the latter part of the year. You can buy the chestnut flour in good delicatessens. Remember that it will only keep a maximum of six months, so make sure it is within date.

SERVES 4

PASTA
300g fresh chestnut flour
100g fine semolina
3 medium-size eggs

SAUCE
30g dried *porcini*, rehydrated
2 garlic cloves, peeled and finely chopped
6 tbsp olive oil
200g button mushrooms, finely sliced
½ tsp chopped fresh hot red chilli (optional)
salt and pepper, to taste
2 tbsp finely chopped fresh flat-leaf parsley

TO FINISH
60g Parmesan, freshly grated.

Soak the dried *porcini* in hot water for 20 minutes. Drain and finely chop. Set aside.

Make the pasta as described on page 30, and roll out and cut into tagliatelle. You can also use dried chestnut tagliatelle if you can find it (but this will be difficult).

Start the sauce by frying the garlic in the olive oil in a large saucepan. Add the sliced mushrooms immediately and cook for about 6 minutes, then add the *porcini*, chilli if you like, and a few tbsp of water. Season with salt and pepper to taste, then add the parsley.

Cook the tagliatelle in plenty of boiling salted water for about 3 minutes or until *al dente*. Drain, mix with the sauce, and serve, sprinkled with the Parmesan.

Maltagliati con Radicchio e Speck

{ Pasta Pieces with Radicchio and Speck }

The idea for this dish, which I have adapted, originates in the Treviso province of Veneto, where the famous *spadone*, a variety of radicchio, grows. The plant undergoes various processes before being sold. For instance, after the whole plant has been plucked from the ground and the leaves bound together, the roots are placed in running fresh water, which takes away a certain bitterness. It is called *radicchio tardivo di Treviso* because it is available during the winter season. There are numerous ways of using radicchio: as a vegetable, in salads, and in risotto. It can even be used to make grappa!

SERVES 4

300g fresh egg pasta (see page 29)
salt and pepper, to taste
50g aged Asiago cheese or Parmesan,
    freshly grated

SAUCE
6 tbsp olive oil
1 onion, peeled and finely chopped
200g Speck, or any smoked bacon or ham, cut
    into small chunks
400g winter radicchio, leaves cut
    into small 6–8cm chunks,
    the roots into small cubes
100ml Prosecco

First of all, roll out the pasta dough, by hand or machine, to 2mm in thickness. Cut into maltagliati (see page 36). Cover with a tea towel until ready to cook.

Heat the oil in a large pan, add the onion and Speck, and fry for a couple of minutes. Add the radicchio and wine plus about 50ml water. Fry until the radicchio is soft, about 10–15 minutes.

Meanwhile, cook the pasta in plenty of boiling salted water for about 4–5 minutes or until *al dente*. Drain the pasta, and mix with the sauce in the pan. Serve sprinkled with the grated cheese and salt and pepper.

ALTERNATIVES

You could use any fresh pasta, particularly long pasta such as tagliatelle. Instead of fresh pasta, you could use 250g dried lasagne or pappardelle, broken into irregular pieces: these would need cooking for about 8 minutes. Red instead of white wine would add a different, deeper flavour, and of course you could scatter the finished dish with some greenery, such as parsley.

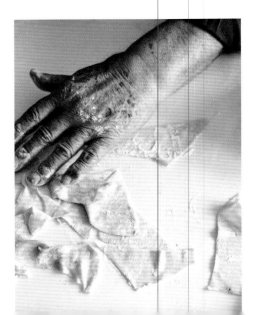

Ravioloni Verdi con Burrata

{ Large Green Ravioli Stuffed with Burrata }

This is the time to show a little skill. *Burrata* is an extremely delicate and soft mozzarella made from cow's milk in Puglia: it is said to have been invented in the 20th century as a means of using up the *ritagli* (scraps or rags) of mozzarella. An outer layer of ordinary mozzarella encloses these scraps of mozzarella mixed with cream, giving it the most wonderful flavour and texture. For this you require freshly made pasta with spinach to give wonderful colour (see page 31).

SERVES 4–6 (MAKING 12 RAVIOLONI)

400g fresh green pasta (see page 29 and 31)
salt and pepper, to taste
80g Parmesan, freshly grated

FILLING AND SAUCE
600g *burrata* mozzarella cheese
50g Parmesan, freshly grated
60g unsalted butter
20g pine kernels, toasted
1 tbsp fresh rosemary needles

Roll out your pasta, by hand or machine, into two long sheets, roughly 15–20cm wide, 2mm thick. Place on your work surface. Cut the *burrata* into 12 pieces. Put half of the pieces evenly along one side of one sheet of pasta, and sprinkle with some of the Parmesan. Wet all round the pieces of cheese with water and fold over the other side of the pasta sheet. Cover the six morsels by pressing the dough all around each to expel the air. Cut into rectangles with a pasta wheel. Cover with a tea towel while making the remainder. Repeat with the other pasta sheet, using the rest of the *burrata* pieces and the remaining Parmesan.

Cook the ravioli gently in plenty of boiling salted water for 2–3 minutes or until *al dente*. Melt the butter in a pan with the pine kernels and rosemary. Let the hot butter absorb the herb flavour for 2 minutes. Scoop the ravioloni out of the water and place in the pan with the melted butter and pine kernels. Serve the pasta in warmed plates, sprinkled with Parmesan.

Raviolo con Sorpresa

{ Surprise Giant Raviolo }

It took me only one glance to steal this idea (yes, this happens sometimes) from the chef of the legendary San Domenico restaurant in Imola about twenty-five years ago. I used to serve this dish in my Neal Street Restaurant some twenty years ago, with the addition of truffle, and ex-customers of the restaurant still remember it with pleasure. Obviously, you will have to make fresh pasta.

SERVES 4

½ recipe fresh egg pasta (see page 29)
salt and pepper, to taste
40g Parmesan, freshly grated

FILLING
600g fresh spinach
300g mascarpone or ricotta cheese
15g Parmesan, freshly grated
a pinch of freshly grated nutmeg
4 bright yellow egg yolks
    (from very fresh, ideally organic eggs)

SAUCE
50g unsalted butter
10 fresh sage leaves

ALTERNATIVES
You could use anything you like as the filling, along with the egg yolk. A cooked fish mixture would be nice, and a particular favourite of mine is sautéed pork sausage mixed with cooked shredded Brussels sprouts...

Roll out the pasta dough, by hand or machine, to 2mm thickness. Cut out 8 circles of 11cm in diameter (this is easy if you have a bowl the right size). Cover with a tea towel until ready to use and cook.

Prepare the filling by boiling the spinach very briefly in salted water. Drain very well (squeezing to get out as much water as possible), then cool and chop very finely. Mix this in a bowl with the mascarpone, Parmesan and nutmeg. Put into a piping bag.

Make a circle of filling with the piping bag on the centre of one pasta circle, leaving enough space in the middle for the egg yolk. Squeeze another circle of filling on top of the first, still leaving the space for the egg yolk. Together these should be about 1.5cm high. Place the egg yolk, very carefully, in the space left for it. Brush the pasta with water all around the filling. Place a second circle of pasta on top and gently press around to bond the sheets together without squashing the centre, or use a fork. You will have a giant raviolo. Repeat with the remaining pasta circles and filling, to make four giant ravioli in all.

Cook the ravioli by gently placing in a large pan of boiling salted water – one or two at a time – and simmering for 5 minutes. After this time the pasta will be cooked and the egg yolk still soft.

Put the butter and sage leaves in a small frying pan and heat gently until the butter foams. Put one raviolo on to a warmed plate, pour the hot foaming butter on top. Season and then sprinkle with some Parmesan. The surprise is the 'explosion' of the brightly coloured yolk when you tuck in with your fork.

Agnolotti del Plin in Tovagliolo

{ Pleated Ravioli in a Napkin }

In the Neal Street Restaurant this was always the dish to draw the attention of the guests. Pasta served in a napkin? What about the sauce? Plin ravioli are very representative of the good food of the Piedmontese: the filling is pleasant, and you just have to toss the ravioli in a pan glazed with juices from the beef roasting tray. It is an invention of my own to serve it in an immaculate starched white napkin, which demonstrates that you don't really need much sauce when you cook delicious pasta. I know you are thinking of your napkins – make this recipe when you want to show off!

SERVES 4

300g fresh egg pasta (see page 29)
salt and pepper, to taste

FILLING
200g spinach leaves, washed and blanched
250g leftover roast beef, cut into small chunks
30g Parmesan, freshly grated
a pinch of freshly grated nutmeg
1 egg yolk

SAUCE
juices from the beef roasting tray
a knob of unsalted butter

Boil the spinach briefly in salted water for 5 minutes. Drain, cool and squeeze out all the moisture. Put the meat, spinach, Parmesan and nutmeg into a blender and blend to make a paste. Taste for salt and pepper and stir in the egg yolk to combine.

Roll out the pasta dough, by hand or machine, to a sheet 2mm thick. Cut into a band or bands 6–7cm wide and as long as you can. Place little piles of the meat and spinach paste at 1cm intervals just below the middle of each strip (see opposite). Close by folding over the other long side of the pasta over the paste, just as if making ordinary ravioli. But now pinch together the dough between the piles of filling to seal the pasta, then cut with the pastry cutter wheel to form the pleated ravioli.

Heat the juices from the beef roasting tray in a small saucepan, and melt the butter into them.

Cook the ravioli in plenty of boiling salted water for 5–6 minutes or until *al dente*. Drain and toss gently in the minimal sauce, just to coat each side of the ravioli. Put four white napkins on four warmed plates, open them out and divide the ravioli between them. Cover the ravioli with the overlapping cloth, and serve.

Raviolo Aperto con Funghi

{ Open Mushroom Raviolo }

I always cook this dish when I come back from a mushroom hunt in the autumn. My booty will be varied – there are many types of edible wild mushrooms, differing in shape, colour and taste – but my greatest preference is for ceps, or *porcini* mushrooms. Should you not be able to collect wild mushrooms, don't be discouraged from making it, as you can nowadays buy a great choice of cultivated 'exotic' mushrooms which make for an acceptable substitution.

SERVES 4

½ recipe fresh egg pasta (see page 29)
salt and pepper, to taste
olive oil
50g unsalted butter
30g Parmesan, freshly grated

FILLING

20g dried *porcini*, rehydrated
500g mixed wild fresh mushrooms, such as
    porcini, chanterelles, bay boletus etc.
50ml olive oil
2 garlic cloves, peeled and finely chopped
2 tbsp chopped fresh flat-leaf parsley

ALTERNATIVES

You could obviously use any filling you desire, from meat, to fish, to vegetable. What is important is the taste… When you have a mixture of fresh and dried mushrooms as here, you can add extra flavour with *porcini* cubes (available in good supermarkets).

Roll out the pasta, by hand or machine, to 1mm thick, and cut out eight 15cm squares. Cover with a tea towel until ready to cook. Soak the dried *porcini* in hot water for 20 minutes. Drain and finely chop.

Clean the fresh mushrooms carefully, wiping rather than washing them. Heat the oil in a large saucepan and gently fry the garlic for a few minutes – you don't want it to brown. Add the fresh and dried mushrooms and some salt and pepper, and stir-fry until the mushrooms are slightly soft, about 7–8 minutes. Add the parsley.

Meanwhile, plunge the sheets of pasta into plenty of boiling salted water to which you have added a little olive oil to prevent the sheets from sticking together. Cook for 3–4 minutes, then lift the pasta out, sheet by sheet. Divide the first four sheets between four warmed plates.

Put a quarter of the mushroom mixture in the centre of these pasta sheets, and cover with the remaining four pasta sheets. It's like covering them with a blanket, don't press.

Add the butter to the mushroom cooking pan, let it melt and foam, and pour over the top of each raviolo. Sprinkle with Parmesan and serve immediately.

Ravioli di Cervo Speziato

{ Spicy Ravioli of Venison }

I used to use lots of venison in The Neal Street Restaurant, mainly as a raw carpaccio with truffle. By using the whole fillet, I would be left with some trimmings, which I would cook and turn into a variety of fillings for stuffed pasta. I believe you shouldn't throw anything away, and always try to make the best of any leftovers. This type of recipe is very characteristic of northern Italy, where wild deer are enthusiastically hunted.

SERVES 4

350g fresh egg pasta (see page 29)
60g Parmesan, freshly grated
salt and pepper, to taste

FILLING
60ml olive oil
2 shallots, peeled and finely sliced
300g lean venison meat, in one piece, or trimmings, cut into small chunks
½ tsp freshly grated nutmeg
a pinch of ground cinnamon
½ tsp paprika, not too hot
40ml strong red wine
150g *mortadella* sausage, cubed

SAUCE
60g unsalted butter
2 tbsp balsamic vinegar

ALTERNATIVES

Use any game birds like grouse, pheasant or wild duck, or any other game animal. *Mortadella* is an Italian sausage, but is available in most good delicatessens.

Heat the oil in a large saucepan and fry the shallots for 3 minutes. Add the venison and let it brown all over before adding the spices and wine. Bring to the boil, and simmer for 10 minutes until the meat is cooked.

Now strain the meat and everything else, keeping the liquid juices. Put the solids in a blender with the *mortadella* and blend to make a soft paste. Pour the juices into a small pan and add the butter and balsamic vinegar. Melt together to make a smooth sauce. Season to taste with salt and pepper, and set aside.

Roll out the pasta dough, by hand or machine, to 1mm thickness. Make the ravioli by hand (see page 142 and page 152) or using a *raviolatrice* (see page 26).

Cook the pasta in plenty of boiling salted water for 5–6 minutes or until *al dente*. Meanwhile, heat the sauce through gently. Drain the pasta and add to the pan with the sauce. Mix well, divide between warmed plates, and serve sprinkled with Parmesan.

Tortelli di Zucca

{ Pumpkin Ravioli }

This speciality comes mainly from Cremona in Lombardy, and it offers
a union of sweet and savoury which is unique in Italian gastronomy.
Based on the very humble pumpkin, the other ingredients of the ravioli
– the almond-flavoured biscuits, known as *Amaretti* and the sweet-sour
preserved *mostarda* fruits – offer a delightfully rich contrast.

SERVES 4

300g fresh egg pasta (see page 29)
salt and pepper, to taste
60g Parmesan, freshly grated

FILLING
550g orange-fleshed pumpkin
olive oil
100g *Amaretti* biscuits (ideally *Amaretti di
    Saronno*), crumbled
100g *mostarda di Cremona* fruits, cut into
    small cubes

SAUCE
80g unsalted butter
10 fresh sage leaves

Preheat the oven to 200°C/Gas 6. Cut the pumpkin into medium-
sized pieces, and place in a roasting tray. Sprinkle with a little oil,
and roast in the oven for about 30 minutes or until soft. Spoon the
flesh from the skin, which you discard, and purée the flesh.

Mix the pumpkin pulp (which mustn't be too wet) with the
crumbled *Amaretti* and the chopped *mostarda* fruits to obtain a
chunky paste.

Roll out the pasta dough, by hand or machine, to a thin sheet 1mm
thick and cut out 32 circles of pasta 6cm in diameter. Put a little
of the filling, about 1 tsp, in the centre of half the circles. Place the
remaining circles on top and press around the border to seal them
well. Wetting the borders with water helps to make it stick. The
result will be 16 tortelli (4 per person).

Cook the pasta in plenty of boiling salted water for 5–6 minutes or
until *al dente*. Meanwhile, melt the butter until foaming in a small
pan, along with the sage leaves. Drain the tortelli, and toss them
with the butter and sage. Divide between warmed plates and serve
sprinkled with grated Parmesan.

Cappelletti Imbottiti di Mascarpone e Prosciutto con Salsa di Spugnole

{ Cappelletti Stuffed with Mascarpone and Ham with Morel Sauce }

Cappelletti, 'little hats', are very similar to tortellini, but with a larger pasta wing on the side (see page 40). Cream and cooked ham are the usual ingredients for the sauce. By using mascarpone cheese from a tub, which is not usually too soft, along with little cubes of cooked ham for texture, we get a surprisingly pleasant pasta filling. Commercial cappelletti are not the same, as their fillings are not as good as the ones you would make.

SERVES 4

½ recipe fresh egg pasta (see page 29)
salt and pepper, to taste
40g Parmesan, freshly grated

FILLING
200g mascarpone cheese
100g cooked ham, very finely cubed
20g Parmesan, freshly grated
2 tbsp chopped chives

SAUCE
80g unsalted butter
1 tbsp chopped rosemary needles
30g dried morels, soaked in water for an
   hour, rehydrated

Mix the filling ingredients together, and put into the fridge for 30 minutes to become harder.

Roll out the pasta dough, by hand or machine, to 2mm thick. Cut into circles of 8–9cm in diameter. You should get about 30. Put ½ tsp of the mixture from the fridge slightly off centre on each circle of dough. Fold each cappelletto to seal the filling as described on page 40.

Cook the pasta in plenty of boiling salted water for 4 minutes or until *al dente*. Taste for texture and leave in the cooking water. Meanwhile, melt the butter in a pan, add the rosemary and drained morels and let the hot butter absorb the herb flavour for 2 minutes. Scoop the cappelletti from the water and add to the butter. Mix together, and add 2–3 tbsp of the pasta water for moisture. Divide between warmed plates, and sprinkle grated Parmesan over each portion.

Tortelli con Granciporro

{ Pasta Squares Stuffed with Crab }

Sometimes there is confusion in the regions concerning the names and shapes of certain pastas. Tortelli, closely related to tortelloni, are the largest of the family: sometimes they are a flat square parcels, and sometimes they are round with a tummy and a hole in the middle. The regions in contention are Emilia-Romagna and Lombardy. Because the filling here is more appropriate to a coastal region, I will attribute the recipe to Romagna, which has a window on the Adriatic.

SERVES 4 (3 TORTELLI EACH)

200g fresh egg pasta (see page 29)
4 small sprigs fresh dill, chopped, to garnish
salt and pepper, to taste

FILLING
1 large crab, about 1.5kg, freshly boiled
75g mascarpone cheese
1 tsp brandy
2 tbsp finely chopped fresh dill

SAUCE
60g unsalted butter
1g saffron strands or 2 sachets powdered
    saffron

TOASTING SAFFRON

This is the way to deal with saffron strands – which I always prefer to powder (there is less risk of adulteration). Put the saffron strands in the bowl of a kitchen spoon and toast it over a gas flame, the flame under the bowl. This dries the saffron, which is then easy to grind to a powder.

Extract all the meat, white and brown, from the crab, making sure there are no bits of shell left. Mix this with the mascarpone, brandy, dill and some salt and pepper to taste. Keep to one side.

Roll out the pasta dough to 1mm thick, preferably by machine, into 1 or 2 long strips. Place 1 tsp of the filling at intervals in the centre of each strip, wet the edges, and fold over (see page 151). Press to seal, then cut into 7cm squares with a serrated cutter.

Cook the pasta in plenty of boiling salted water for 4–5 minutes or until *al dente*. Meanwhile, melt the butter in a small pan until foaming, then add the saffron. Divide the tortelli between warmed plates, three per portion. Pour some of the saffron butter over the top, and decorate with freshly chopped dill. Serve hot.

Pasta e Cavolo (Krautfleckerl)

{ Pasta and Cabbage }

When I moved to Vienna to continue my studies, I had to find my way around the new cultural food scene. Maria, the mother of my girlfriend, was a great cook, particularly of all those recipes of Bohemian and Hungarian cuisine, which form a great part of Viennese cooking. The Krautfleckerl drew my attention because of its simplicity: basically it uses little squares of pasta, which can be bought dried, rather like the Italian quadrucci. This dish can be eaten by itself or used as an accompaniment to a roast or stewed meat.

SERVES 4

300g fresh egg pasta (see page 29)

SAUCE
80g lard or 70ml vegetable oil
1 medium onion, peeled and finely sliced
600–700g firm, white cabbage, cut from the
    centre, no stalk, cut into small pieces
1 tsp caraway seeds
1 tbsp caster sugar
1 tbsp strong white wine vinegar
salt and pepper, to taste

Melt the lard in a large saucepan, and add the onion. Fry it slowly for about 6 minutes to soften. Now add the cabbage and caraway seeds and cook for about 5–10 minutes, stirring frequently. Add the sugar and about 2 tbsp water, and continue to cook, stirring from time to time, until the cabbage softens, about 15 minutes. Add the vinegar and continue to cook until you obtain a thickish pale brown sauce, another 5 minutes or so. Add salt and pepper to taste, and continue to let it cook slowly.

Make the quadrucci as described on page 36, and set aside.

Cook the pasta in plenty of boiling salted water for 6 minutes or until *al dente*. Drain and add to the sauce. Mix well and serve. No cheese!

Agnolotti di Maiale con Cavolini

{ Pasta Squares with a Pork and Brussels Sprout Filling }

It was when I was a guest of the Naylor-Leyland family near Peterborough that I had the idea for making this pasta filling from what food they had leftover in their kitchen. Pasta fillings are often made from other dishes. You just have to let your imagination and passion work. These particular little pasta parcels turned out to be delicious, according to the other guests!

SERVES 4

500g fresh egg pasta (see page 29)
salt and pepper, to taste
60g Parmesan, freshly grated

FILLING
2 tbsp olive oil
400g minced pork, or pure pork sausage meat
2 garlic cloves, peeled and chopped
200g cooked Brussels sprouts, left over from
    a previous meal
½ tsp freshly grated nutmeg
20g Parmesan, freshly grated

SAUCE
80g unsalted butter
1 sprig fresh rosemary
1 tbsp balsamic vinegar

Heat the oil in a large saucepan, and fry the mince and garlic until brown, about 10 minutes. Remove from the pan and leave to cool. When cool, place in the goblet of your food processor and add the Brussels sprouts, nutmeg and Parmesan. Blend to obtain a paste. Taste for salt and pepper and set aside.

Roll out the pasta dough, by hand or machine, to a longish sheet of about 1.5mm thick. Make ravioli of about 2.5cm square, by hand (see pages 142 or 152), or using the *raviolatrice* (follow instructions page 26).

Cook the pasta in plenty of boiling salted water for 5–6 minutes or until *al dente*. Melt the butter in a large saucepan, then add the rosemary and vinegar, and allow the butter to absorb the flavours for 2 minutes. Drain the pasta and add to the butter. Remove the rosemary. Toss to coat well. Divide the pasta between warmed plates and sprinkle with Parmesan.

Tajarin con Animelle e Fegatini
{ Pasta Ribbons with Sweetbreads and Chicken Livers }

Tajarin, the local name for very thin hand-cut tagliolini, are the pride of Piedmont. They are eaten with truffles, in a soup with dumplings (see page 55) or with the sauce I suggest here. However you eat them, they are delicious.

SERVES 4

300g fresh egg pasta (see page 29)
salt and pepper, to taste
50g Parmesan, freshly grated

SAUCE
200g veal sweetbreads
40ml olive oil
40g unsalted butter
1 onion, peeled and very finely chopped
300g chicken livers, cleaned and cut into
    small chunks
2 tsp balsamic vinegar
2 tbsp finely chopped fresh flat-leaf parsley

Roll out the pasta dough, by hand or machine, to $\frac{1}{2}$mm thickness. Roll and cut into ribbons (see page 33). Coil and leave to dry a little while you make the sauce.

To start the sauce, plunge the sweetbreads into boiling salted water for a few seconds. Remove from the water, cut away any sinew, and cut the flesh into small ribbons.

Heat the oil and butter together in a large saucepan and sauté the onion for 2 minutes. Add the chicken livers and sweetbreads and stir-fry for 5 minutes. Add the balsamic vinegar and parsley, and taste for salt and pepper.

Cook the pasta in plenty of boiling salted water for 3–4 minutes or until *al dente*. Lift from the water using tongs and put straight into the pan with the sauce. Mix well and divide between warmed plates. Serve with a sprinkling of grated Parmesan.

Culurgiones

{ Plaited Sardinian Ravioli }

Every region has some sort of stuffed pasta on the menu, which is often made in order to use up leftovers. Sardinia has a different kind of stuffed pasta, a so-called raviolo whose filling can vary from potato to cheese. Also known as culurzones (and a number of other names), these ravioli even look different from those of other regions. They are delightful anyway, despite the fact that a little more work is involved.

SERVES 4

1 recipe fresh egg pasta (see page 29)
salt and pepper, to taste
60g pecorino cheese, freshly grated

FILLING
30g unsalted butter
200g spinach, blanched, squeezed dry
    and finely chopped
300g fresh ricotta cheese
2 medium eggs, beaten
80g pecorino cheese, freshly grated
1 sachet powdered saffron
a pinch of ground cinnamon

SAUCE
50ml olive oil
1 small onion, peeled and finely sliced
120g minced beef
120g minced lean pork
50ml dry Vernaccia white wine
500g canned crushed tomatoes
2 tbsp finely chopped fresh flat-leaf parsley
1 tbsp finely chopped fresh sage leaves

Make the filling by melting the butter in a wide pan, and frying the dry squeezed spinach for a few minutes. Let it cool, then add the ricotta, beaten eggs, grated pecorino, saffron and the cinnamon. Season with salt and pepper to taste, and work everything thoroughly together to a well-mixed paste.

Meanwhile, make the sauce. First of all, heat the oil in a large saucepan and fry the onion for about 5 minutes to soften. Add the two meats and brown a little, about 5 minutes, then add the Vernaccia followed by the tomatoes, parsley and sage. Cook slowly for 30 minutes, then taste for salt and pepper.

Meanwhile, roll the pasta dough out thinly, by hand or machine, to 1mm thickness, and cut into 8cm circles. Make and fill the culurgiones following the instructions on page 41.

Cook the pasta in plenty of boiling salted water for 4 minutes or until *al dente*. Drain, mix with the sauce and serve sprinkled with pecorino.

Bigoli con l'Anara (Anatra)
{ Thick Spaghetti with Duck Sauce }

The Veneto is known more for its cooking of rice rather than its cooking of pasta. One of the few pastas associated with Venice and the Veneto are bigoli, a handmade extruded pasta made with a small machine called a *bigolaro*. This is a metal cylinder with a die at the end through which the dough is pushed. The resulting pasta is a large spaghetti 3mm in diameter, with a hole in the middle. The best way to eat them is either *in salsa*, with an anchovy and onion sauce, or with an *anara* (duck or, even better, the giblets of duck) sauce. But you can also make the bigoli at home without a machine (see page 33), but they will have a square instead of a round profile – and no hole in the middle!

SERVES 4

1 recipe fresh egg pasta (see page 29)
salt and pepper, to taste
60g Parmesan, freshly grated
a good pinch of freshly grated nutmeg

SAUCE
50g unsalted butter
50ml olive oil
1 onion, finely chopped
1 tbsp fresh rosemary needles, plus extra
    to garnish
300g duck giblets, the liver, heart and gizzard,
    all finely chopped, kept separate
60ml red wine

For the sauce, heat the butter and oil together in a large saucepan, add the onion and rosemary and fry until the onion is soft, about 5 minutes. Add the chopped duck gizzard and heart and stir-fry for 10 minutes. Add the livers and red wine and cook for another 10 minutes. Season with salt and pepper to taste.

Roll out the pasta, by hand or machine, to 2–4mm thick, and cut as described on page 33.

Cook the pasta in plenty of boiling salted water for 8–10 minutes or until *al dente*. Drain, add to the sauce and mix well. Divide between warmed plates and serve sprinkled with grated Parmesan, chopped rosemary needles and a good grating of nutmeg.

Gnocchi di Patate al Pesto

{ Potato and Flour Dumplings with Pesto }

Many people try to make gnocchi without managing to achieve the perfect softness and lightness of a cloud. To have a perfect plate of gnocchi, which are also very good with a tomato sauce (see page 67), follow this recipe exactly. Here I suggest you add *quagliata* or junket to make a pesto popular in the eastern parts of Liguria, but you could leave this out.

SERVES 4

GNOCCHI
800g floury potatoes
200g Italian '00' flour
1 medium egg
salt and pepper, to taste
60g Parmesan cheese, freshly grated

SAUCE
1 recipe fresh pesto (see page 69)
2 tbsp *quagliata* (curdled milk), crème fraîche or junket (optional)

ALTERNATIVES

You can make green gnocchi just as you can green pasta. For this amount of gnocchi mixture, add 300g cooked spinach, drained and squeezed very dry. Mix into the basic gnocchi dough, adding more flour if the mixture seems too wet.

These gnocchi are also delicious with a blue cheese and spinach sauce. Just melt 30g of butter in a pan, add 150g Gorgonzola dolce cheese, broken into small pieces, and stir and dilute with milk as required. Add 250g spinach leaves and leave them to wilt, at which point the sauce is ready.

Preheat the oven to 200°C/Gas 6. Pierce the potatoes a few times with a knife, place in the oven and bake for 1 hour until tender. Scoop the cooked flesh out into a bowl and mash to a purée. Do not use a machine, as this makes the potato too sticky. Mix the potato purée with the flour and egg. Work it together, kneading with your hands, until it is a homogeneous mixture. Taking a little at a time from the pile of dough, form it on a floured work surface into sausage shapes 2cm in diameter. Cut 2cm chunks with a knife then lightly press, away from you, against the tines of an upright fork to get ridge indentations. (These will help to collect more sauce.) Place the finished gnocchi on a clean pre-floured cloth.

Meanwhile, make the pesto as described on page 69, adding the curdled milk, or junket if you like. When finished, put it in a saucepan big enough to hold the gnocchi and add a little water. The sauce has to remain raw although warm, so heat it through very, very gently.

Cook the gnocchi in plenty of boiling salted water. After 30 seconds to 1 minute the gnocchi will swim up to the surface of the water. They are now cooked. Scoop them out with a slotted spoon and put into the pan with the pesto. Mix well, season to taste and serve immediately with a sprinkling of grated Parmesan.

Passatelli con Involtini di Bue/ Rindsrouladen und Spätzle

{ Beef Olives with Dumplings }

This dish is in honour of Sabine, my partner in happiness, who was born in Germany and is the perfect executor of this typical German dish with Spätzle, an instantly made pasta. The pasta is also found in the north-east corner of Italy, where the gastronomic culture is a bit more German. The Italian passatelli are made and cooked more or less in the same way.

SERVES 4 (MAKES 4 BEEF OLIVES)

DUMPLINGS
450g Italian '00' flour
4 medium eggs
130ml sparkling mineral water

BEEF OLIVES
4 large thin slices of beef topside,
    5mm thick and about 15cm long,
    10cm wide
1 tbsp Dijon mustard
1 small onion, peeled and finely chopped
8 rashers smoked streaky bacon
4 small dill-pickled gherkins, cut into strips
    lengthways
plain flour, for coating
50ml olive oil

SAUCE
2 carrots, peeled and cut into small chunks
1 leek, cleaned and cut into slices
100ml red wine
beef stock (see page 47), to cover
salt and pepper, to taste
a knob of unsalted butter
    (optional, but I like it)

ALTERNATIVES
You can of course serve the sauce with potatoes or normal gnocchi (see page 164).

Mix together the flour, eggs and mineral water to make a soft dough for the dumplings, cover with a tea towel, and set aside.

Put the four slices of meat on to a work surface and spread the mustard thinly on each. Cover with the onion, then lay two slices of bacon lengthways on it. At right angles place the strips of gherkin. Roll each beef olive up and secure with kitchen string, taking care to seal well. Dust with flour and fry in the oil in a large pan to brown each side. Remove and set aside.

Add the carrots and leek to the same pan and fry a little in the remaining oil, then add the wine and let the alcohol evaporate for 2 minutes. Place the beef olives in the pan, cover with the beef stock (if necessary you can use stock cubes), and cook slowly for $1\frac{1}{2}$ hours.

Just before serving take out the meat and liquidise the sauce. Adjust the seasoning with salt and pepper. My personal input at this stage, is to add a knob of butter.

When ready to serve, bring a large saucepan of slightly salted water to the boil, and lay across the top a Spätzle or passatelli gadget. Put only part of the dough on this at a time, and with a spatula force the dough through the holes to let pasta pellets drop into the water. Repeat until all the dough is used up. The Spätzle will be cooked when they bob to the surface, probably within about 3 minutes. Scoop them out with a slotted spoon, and drain well. (Or, in the absence of a special gadget, the large holes on a grater will work – just use a knife to cut the Spätzle off into 5mm chunks. However, the dough needs to be stiffer.)

Mix the pasta with the sauce, cut the beef olives into thick slices and arrange them on the top to serve.

PASTA AL FORNO
BAKED PASTA

Italian food is usually so simple in terms of ingredients, and in terms of cooking technique, that you might wonder why we would ever bother to make a more elaborate timbale or pie, which takes everything that stage further!

The answer, of course, is that baking the ingredients together produces a richer, more opulent dish, which is precisely what you need when you are entertaining guests, whether family or friends. In the famous Italian novel *Il Gattopardo* (*The Leopard*) by Giuseppe Tomasi di Lampedusa, which chronicles the changes in Sicilian life and society during the *Risorgimento*, the unification of Italy in the 19th century. The Leopard himself organised the baking of a macaroni pie for his special guests once a year. With a little bit of extra effort, you can simulate his baronial Sicilian dish (see page 177). The results will completely justify the time and effort, which will please all your guests. It will please you too, because once all the preparation is done, all you have to do is put the pasta dish in the oven. You can then join the party until the dish is ready!

One of the best characteristics of baked pasta pies is that while the separate internal layers stay soft and moist, a fantastic crispness develops on top from cooking in the oven... The contrasting textures of the finished dish are wonderful.

Pasticcio di Ziti e Verdure

{ Vegetable Bake with Thick Pasta Tubes }

'Ti sei messo in un bel pasticcio,' is what they say in Italy, when you get yourself in a mess, and I would obviously prefer to eat a *pasticcio* than be in one! This particular dish is made with a pasta much loved by Neapolitans. Ziti are hollow tubes of pasta, 1cm in diameter, and ranging from 10–40cm in length. The short one is the main actor in this dish which, unusually, instead of sauce, has juicy chunks of vegetables.

SERVES 4–6

400g dried short ziti pasta
salt and pepper, to taste

FILLING
400g yellow and red bell peppers, deseeded
    and cut into strips
olive oil, for frying
3 garlic cloves, peeled and halved
2 tsp white wine vinegar
400g aubergine, cut into thick slices
    and cubed
300g courgettes, cut into 1cm slices
2 large onions, peeled and cut into thick slices
a little freshly grated nutmeg
500g buffalo mozzarella cheese, sliced
    and cubed
150g Parmesan, freshly grated

Preheat the oven to 180°C/Gas 4.

First cut the peppers in half and deseed them, then cut into strips. Fry these strips in 1 tbsp olive oil until the edges are blackening. At this point add the garlic and fry for a few more minutes. Add some salt to taste then the white wine vinegar, and set aside.

Now cut the aubergine first into thick slices and then into cubes. Put these in water so they don't absorb too much oil later, about 10 minutes. Drain, and fry the cubes in 2 tbsp olive oil until soft and caramelising, about 10 minutes. Cut the courgettes in 1cm slices and fry in 2 tsp olive oil until brown on both sides. Cut the onions in thick slices and fry in 6 tbsp olive oil until browned on both sides, about 10 minutes. Put the vegetables and their oils, plus the nutmeg, into a suitable ovenproof dish. Cut the mozzarella in slices and then into cubes.

Cook the ziti in plenty of boiling salted water for 8–10 minutes or until *al dente*. Drain and mix together with the vegetables and their oils. Intersperse with the mozzarella and most of the Parmesan, which should melt with the heat of the pasta and season to taste with salt and pepper. Finish with a sprinkle of the remaining Parmesan.

Put into the preheated oven and bake for about 20 minutes. Serve hot.

Cannelloni Ripieni di Funghi con Salsa di Taleggio e Tartufi

{ Stuffed Cannelloni with Taleggio and Truffle Sauce }

Cannelloni are very large pasta tubes, which are cooked in water until very *al dente*, then stuffed with whatever filling is desired, along with a white or tomato sauce, and grated Parmesan. Then they are baked. It's one of the classic *pasta al forno* dishes, but the industry of ready-cooked meals has made me lose my desire for it. Once on the train to Manchester, the dining car was offering cannelloni. I asked them to show me the packaging and it said that its contents could be kept for two years and still be edible! That's why I don't care for it much any more, apart from homemade.

SERVES 4

½ recipe fresh egg pasta dough (see page 29)
salt and pepper, to taste
a few drops of olive oil
unsalted butter, for greasing
60g Parmesan, freshly grated

SAUCE
300g Taleggio cheese, cut into small pieces
50ml milk
2 medium egg yolks
a few drops of truffle oil (optional)
50g black truffle, very finely sliced

FILLING
20g dried *porcini,* rehydrated
60ml extra virgin olive oil
2 garlic cloves, peeled and finely chopped
a little chopped fresh red chilli, not too hot
700g mixed wild mushrooms, cleaned and cut into medium slices

ALTERNATIVES
You can use eight tubes of dried cannelloni, but you will have to cook these first before stuffing (follow the instructions on the packet). The sauce and filling above are vegetarian, but you could choose a meat filling (one of the *ragùs* from pages 98–108 would do), with a different sauce on top (a white sauce, for instance, see page 180), perhaps with some grated cheese added.

Start the sauce first. In a medium saucepan, soak the Taleggio pieces in the milk for a few hours.

Preheat the oven to 180°C/Gas 4. Soak the dried *porcini* for the filling in hot water for 20 minutes, then drain and chop.

Heat the oil in a large frying pan and fry the garlic and chilli for a few minutes, but don't let them brown. Add the drained chopped *porcini* and fry for 1 minute. Add the fresh sliced mushrooms and stir-fry with a little salt until they are almost soft, about 5 minutes. Remove from the heat and set aside.

Roll the pasta out until 2mm thick, either by hand or in the pasta machine. Cut into eight 15cm squares. Plunge the pasta into a pan of boiling salted water with a few drops of oil and cook for a minute before draining and arranging on your work surface.

Divide the filling between the part-cooked pasta squares, arranging it along one end of each piece of pasta. Roll it up with the filling inside, and put in a suitable greased baking dish, join side down (see page 170).

Put the cheese and milk for the sauce on a very low heat, and stir to melt the cheese into the milk, to make a cream. Stir the yolks in carefully, you don't want them to curdle. Stir in the truffle oil, if using, and the truffle, setting aside a few slices.

Pour the sauce over the cannelloni, sprinkle with the Parmesan, pepper and top with the remaining truffle slices. Bake in the preheated oven for 20 minutes. Serve hot.

Pizzoccheri della Valtellina

{ Baked Buckwheat Noodles with Cheese, Courgettes and Potato }

This classic recipe from the valley near Milan is made in various versions. Sometimes the noodles are served just with cabbage and potatoes, sometimes with added spinach. I have also tried it with courgettes and potatoes, as here, and it works very well. The most important thing is the pizzoccheri, which are noodles made from buckwheat flour. You can make these fresh – if you can find the flour – or buy them dried in a packet, they look like short tagliatelle. They come from the Valtellina valley, which also has a very good semi-hard cow's milk cheese, *Bitto*. (Bresaola, the cured beef, also comes from the Valtellina.)

SERVES 4

PASTA AL FORNO

300g dried pizzoccheri pasta
300g courgettes, trimmed and cubed
300g waxy potatoes, peeled and cubed
salt and pepper, to taste
200g *Bitto* cheese, or *Fontina* or *Toma*, cut into small cubes
60g unsalted butter
80g Parmesan, freshly grated
2 garlic cloves, peeled and finely sliced

Preheat the oven to 180°C/Gas 4.

Put the pasta, courgettes and potatoes into a large saucepan full of boiling salted water, and cook until everything is tender, about 12 minutes.

Drain well, then mix with the *Bitto* cheese, 40g of the butter and 60g of the Parmesan. Put in a suitable ovenproof dish. Sprinkle with the remaining Parmesan and bake in the preheated oven for about 20 minutes.

Meanwhile, melt the remaining butter in a pan with the sliced garlic and heat until foaming. Remove the pizzoccheri from the oven and spoon over the melted garlic butter and season with salt and pepper. Serve hot. A good glass of *Sassella* red wine will be complementary.

ALTERNATIVES

You could replace the courgettes with the more traditional cabbage, or you could use spinach or even quartered Brussels sprouts.

Timballo del Gattopardo

{ The Leopard's Macaroni Pie }

I feel privileged to have had something to do with this historical recipe. In 2008 the BBC asked me to present a TV programme to investigate the food liked and written about by Giuseppe di Tomasi di Lampedusa, a prince of Sicily, born at the end of the 19th century. This noble Sicilian was the writer of the most successful novel of Italian literature, *Il Gattopardo (The Leopard)*, which is still very much admired today. I cooked in the original kitchen of the Villa di San Marco in Palermo, belonging to friends of the Prince, the family Camerata. The original recipe for this macaroni pie specifies unborn eggs from the ovary of a chicken and truffles. I have replaced these with hard-boiled chicken egg yolks, quails' egg yolks and dried *porcini*.

SERVES 10

1kg dried smooth macaroni
salt and pepper, to taste
2 x packets ready-made shortcrust pastry
unsalted butter, for greasing
flour, for dusting

ROASTING JUICES
1 piece of veal, about 500g
100ml olive oil
300ml dry white wine
1 onion, peeled and finely chopped
1 carrot, peeled and finely chopped
2 celery stalks, finely chopped
1 sprig fresh rosemary

FILLING
50g dried *porcini*, rehydrated
150ml olive oil
2 onions, peeled and finely sliced
400g lean chicken flesh, cut into small chunks
500g chicken livers, cleaned and cut into small chunks
300g chicken hearts, cleaned and cut into small chunks
300g cooked ham, cut into cubes
200ml dry white wine
10 very hard-boiled chicken egg yolks
12 very hard-boiled quails' egg yolks
150g Parmesan, freshly grated

ALTERNATIVE

It's unnecessary to say that this dish should be cooked for a very grand occasion. If you are very rich you can use white truffle instead of the *porcini*, but I am sure *The Leopard* would lick his paws in this version too!

Preheat the oven to 180°C/Gas 4 for the veal cooking and for the pie itself. Soak the dried *porcini* in hot water for 20 minutes. Drain and chop.

Put the piece of veal in a pot-roasting dish with the oil and brown on each side for a few minutes. Add the wine, the vegetables and rosemary, put the lid on and cook slowly in the preheated oven for 1 hour. Collect the cooking juices in a jug, and keep the meat for another meal.

In a large casserole, put 6 tbsp of the oil and fry the onions first until soft, about 10 minutes. Then add the chicken chunks and fry for 7 minutes. Now add the chicken livers and hearts and the soaked *porcini*. Cook for a few minutes, stirring, then add the ham and the wine and cook for 10 minutes until the wine has evaporated a little. Then add the juices from the roast meat, and ultimately all the hard-boiled egg yolks, stirring them in very gently.

Meanwhile, cook the pasta in plenty of boiling salted water for 5–6 minutes until barely *al dente*, then drain.

Roll the shortcrust pastry out on a lightly floured surface until it is about 4mm thick. Use about three-quarters of it to line a large greased dish of about 25cm in diameter, 12cm high. The remaining pastry should be enough for the lid; cover it with a cloth.

Mix the pasta with all the filling and the juices, adding the Parmesan, and pour everything carefully into the pastry-lined pie dish. Cover with the pastry lid, seal at the sides and make a couple of holes in the centre. Brush with a little of the liquid from the sauce, and bake in the preheated oven for 30 minutes. Serve hot.

Trullo di Zitoni

{ Meat and Pasta Pie }

This dish is a tribute to Puglia, and particularly to those ancient Pugliese stone buildings, the *trulli*. These are conical in shape, and were built without cement in order that they could be taken apart and re-erected elsewhere by their nomadic farmer-owners. The zitoni is a long tubular pasta, ideal to build a timbale, in this case in a *trullo* shape. This pasta, slightly wider than ziti, is available at very good Italian delicatessens.

SERVES 6–8

PASTA AL FORNO

400g dried long zitoni pasta
salt and pepper, to taste
olive oil, for brushing

FILLING
2 onions, peeled and finely chopped
2 celery stalks, finely chopped
200g carrots, peeled, cooked until soft, and finely chopped
50ml olive oil
350g minced lean lamb
200g chicken livers, cleaned and coarsely chopped
300g button mushrooms, halved
3 tbsp dry white wine
6 fresh basil leaves
300g aged Caciocavallo cheese, finely cubed
3 medium eggs, beaten

ALTERNATIVE

Any of the sauces in the book, so long as they are not too liquid, could be used. The egg is important as a binder.

Cook the pasta in plenty of boiling salted water for 10–12 minutes or until just *al dente*: you want the shape to remain intact. Drain and sprinkle with a little olive oil to prevent the pasta strands from sticking together.

Start to prepare the filling by first frying the onion, celery and carrots in 50ml olive oil. When soft, after about 5 minutes, add the lamb mince, the chicken livers and the mushrooms. Fry for a few minutes until the mince has browned nicely. Add the wine, basil and salt and pepper to taste, and cook it all together gently for 15 minutes. Finally, just before using, stir in the cheese and beaten eggs. Set aside.

Preheat the oven to 200°C/Gas 6.

Line a pre-oiled, round and deep ovenproof bowl – about 15cm high and 25cm across – with the pasta, covering the entire surface, stacking each coil of the pasta on top of another (as if you were making a coiled basket). Put the filling into the cavity, cover with foil and bake in the preheated oven for 20 minutes. Leave to cool for 10 minutes, then very carefully invert the bowl on to a large flat, ovenproof plate. (You may have to do a little 'mending'!)

Heat your oven grill to near its maximum. Brush the outside of your pasta *trullo* with oil, and return to the hot oven to grill for 10 minutes or until the top of the pasta is crisp and a wonderful golden brown in colour. Serve hot.

Piccolo Vincisgrassi

{ Little Grand Lasagne }

This is a traditional dish of the Marche. The recipe is named for an Austrian-German General called Windisch-Graetz who was passing through the region in 1799 during the Napoleonic rule. The dish – a rich version of lasagne – is still known today as *Vincisgrassi*, the 'maccheronical' translation of his name and – here it is! The original was stuffed full of culinary delights such as chicken livers, giblets, cock's comb... Here I have limited myself to sweetbreads, ceps and truffles, the undisputed luxuries of today...

SERVES 6

400g fresh egg pasta dough (see page 29)
salt and pepper, to taste

FILLING
300g fresh ceps or *porcini*
100g unsalted butter, for frying
200g veal sweetbreads
50g white truffle from Acqualagna,
    though I prefer the one from Alba
50g Parmesan, freshly grated

WHITE SAUCE 'BÉCHAMEL'
50g unsalted butter
50g plain flour
100ml milk
freshly grated nutmeg

ALTERNATIVES

You can of course use this basic idea with a pasta, white sauce, and some *ragù bolognese* (see page 108) to make a less extravagant baked lasagne. If using dried lasagne pasta, you would need to bake the dish for longer.

Preheat the oven to 180°C/Gas 4.

Lightly clean the ceps or *porcini*, then slice them and sauté in half of the butter for a few minutes. Add salt and pepper to taste. Blanch the sweetbreads in boiling water to allow them to stiffen a little (5 minutes). Drain and when cooled a bit, discard the sinew. Cut into slices and fry in the remaining butter, in the same pan as the ceps, until brown.

Make the white sauce or béchamel. Melt the butter, stir in the flour then gradually stir in the milk. Stir constantly until the mixture has a good pouring consistency. Season with nutmeg, salt and pepper.

Roll out the pasta either by machine or with a rolling pin to a thickness of 2mm. Cut into 15cm squares. Plunge the pasta into a pan of boiling salted water with a few drops of oil and cook for a minute before draining and arranging on your work surface.

Build a layer of pasta in a 20–25cm diameter ovenproof dish, cutting the squares to fit. Add some slices of cep, slices of sweetbreads and a few slices of truffle. Cover with some white sauce and sprinkle with grated Parmesan. Repeat, layering everything up, until you have used all your ingredients.

Bake in the preheated oven for 15 minutes, and serve.

Pasta Classica al Forno

{ Southern Celebratory Baked Pasta }

Of all the Italian dishes involving pasta, this super-classic – of which
various regional variations exist – is perhaps the most engaging, and
it's worth every bite. It is normally baked for grand occasions, even for
weddings, and it can be quite rich. But when Italians celebrate they can
eat far more than they imagine out of sheer greed and sheer pleasure. This
dish was usually made by my mother for Easter and Christmas, and it was
always magnificent. We would finish it off the next day, when it tasted even
better! It's ideal for parties as it can be prepared in advance.

SERVES 8–10

1kg dried pasta: choose from large rigatoni
    or penne, mafalde, broken-up long ziti,
    macaroni etc.
salt and pepper, to taste

SAUCE
200ml olive oil
2 onions, peeled and finely sliced
2 garlic cloves, peeled and crushed
2kg canned crushed tomatoes
100g tomato paste
10 fresh basil leaves

MEATBALLS
500g beef mince
30g Parmesan, freshly grated
2 medium eggs, beaten
50g fresh breadcrumbs
1 garlic clove, peeled and crushed
30ml red wine
seed oil for frying, such as peanut or sunflower

LAYERING
1 recipe spinach balls (see page 90)
300g thinly sliced salami, perhaps with
    fennel seeds
600g Taleggio cheese, cut into small chunks
200g Parmesan, freshly grated
12 medium eggs
salt and pepper

Preheat the oven to 180°C/Gas 4.

To make the sauce, heat the oil in a large casserole dish, and fry the
onions and garlic for a few minutes. Add the crushed tomatoes, the
tomato paste and basil and cook slowly for 30 minutes, adding a
little water if necessary.

For the meatballs, put the mince into a bowl and add some salt and
pepper, the Parmesan, the beaten eggs, breadcrumbs, garlic and
wine. Mix well, then make into balls the size of a walnut. Shallow-
fry in seed oil until brown. Set aside.

Make the spinach balls as described on page 90, frying them at the
end in a little of the seed oil, as you did the meatballs.

Cook the pasta now in plenty of boiling salted water for 8 minutes
or until barely *al dente*. Drain and flavour with a little of the sauce.

In a baking dish of about 20–25cm in diameter, start with a layer of
pasta and then add some of the salami, some of the meatballs and
spinach balls, and some of the Taleggio cheese. Spread with some
sauce and grated Parmesan. Build two to three layers in the same
way and finish with lots of Taleggio, sauce and Parmesan. Beat the
eggs with salt and pepper and pour evenly over the top: the liquid
will penetrate to the bottom layer. Bake in the preheated oven for
30 minutes. Take out, let the dish rest for a few minutes, then dig
deep. Delicious…

Sformato di Anelletti

{ Baked Ring Pasta }

Anello is a ring, and in Sicily, this pasta shape is used for baked timbales or pies. These can be eaten warm or cold, and you usually find them in delicatessens but also in bars, which at lunchtime function as *tavola calda* restaurants (literally 'hot table'), where they serve regional dishes.

SERVES 6–8

500g dried anelli pasta
salt and pepper, to taste
unsalted butter, for greasing

FILLING
600g vegetables (mixed peas, celery, carrot, aubergine), diced
4 tbsp olive oil
1 onion, peeled and finely chopped
2 garlic cloves, peeled and crushed
700g pork mince
100g sausage *(luganega)*, skinned
1.5kg canned crushed tomatoes
10 fresh basil leaves
20ml red wine (a splash)
150g Caciocavallo cheese, half cut into small cubes, half grated

Preheat the oven to 180°C/Gas 4.

Start the *ragù* by cutting your prepared vegetables into small dice. Heat the oil in a large saucepan, and fry the onion and garlic for a few minutes until softened. Add the mince, sausage meat and the diced vegetables. Cook for 10–15 minutes, stirring, then add the tomatoes, basil, red wine, and some salt and pepper. Cook for 30 minutes until everything is tender.

Cook the pasta in plenty of boiling salted water for 6–8 minutes or until *al dente*, then drain. Flavour all the pasta with the liquid part of the *ragù*, just enough to give it colour and flavour.

Grease the inside of a baking dish of 25cm at least in diameter, and 8–10cm high with a little butter. This will help the pasta adhere. Line the inside of the dish with most of the pasta, leaving space in the centre for the *ragù*. Pour the relatively dry *ragù* into the centre, and cover with more pasta to seal it completely. Sprinkle and place the cheese over the top, then bake in the preheated oven for 20 minutes. Leave it to cool.

When the pie is cold, invert it on to a plate. It will be solid. It can be eaten cold or reheated. Serve in wedges.

Gnocchi di Semolino alla Romana

{ Baked Semolina Dumplings Roman Style }

This may be a Roman dish, but not only the Romans are fond of it, as it is very homely and comforting. This is yet another version of the classic, which I have made and published many times. Optionally you could accompany the dish with a little simple tomato sauce (see page 67).

SERVES 4–6

750ml milk
salt and pepper, to taste
150g unsalted butter, plus extra for greasing
250g fine semolina
olive oil
2 medium eggs, beaten
150g Parmesan, freshly grated
a pinch of freshly grated nutmeg

Put the milk in a large saucepan and bring to the boil with a pinch of salt and 30g of the butter. Now pour the semolina in slowly, stirring in order to avoid forming lumps, and cook, still stirring, for 20 minutes. Remove from the heat.

Oil your work surface. Beat the eggs in a bowl with 20g of the Parmesan and some salt and pepper.

Before the semolina becomes cold but when it is not still too hot, pour the egg mixture into the semolina pan and mix well. Now pour the semolina on to the oiled surface and spread with a spatula to about 2.5cm in height. Leave to get cold.

Preheat the oven to 180°C/Gas 4.

In the meantime, grease an ovenproof ceramic dish with butter of about 25–28cm long, 20cm wide. When the semolina is cold, cut out discs with a pastry ring 4cm in diameter. Lift these discs out and place in the greased dish, slightly overlapping them, until the dish is filled. Sprinkle with the rest of the Parmesan and the butter and the nutmeg. Bake in the preheated oven for 20–30 minutes until the cheese on top melts and browns. *Buon appetito.*

Anolini con Panna e Prosciutto

{ Little Ham and Cheese Pasta Parcels in Pastry Cases }

For a change, for this recipe you should buy freshly made anolini, which are the smallest size of tortellini. They are made in Emilia-Romagna by hand, usually by women: only women have small enough fingers to turn the little stuffed parcels around. My fingers are far too large!

SERVES 4

600g frozen all-butter puff pastry
plain flour, for dusting
unsalted butter, for greasing
1 medium egg, beaten

FILLING
500g freshly made small anolini or tortellini
    (see pages 29, 40 and 156)
salt and pepper, to taste
50ml double cream
¼ tsp freshly grated nutmeg
100g cooked ham, cut into small strips
50g Parmesan, freshly grated

ALTERNATIVES
If you don't have time to make them, good-quality fresh anolini or tortellini are available from most Italian delicatessens. You could also sprinke the filling with a little chopped fresh chilli and basil before putting the lid on.

Preheat the oven to 180°C/Gas 4.

Roll out the pastry on a lightly floured surface to about 1cm thick. Have four metal or ovenproof bowls ready, 10cm in diameter and 10cm high. Grease the outside of these, and cover them upside down with puff pastry, cutting to fit. Cut four 10cm circles to act as lids. Place the cases and the lids on a greased baking sheet. Brush the outside of the cases and the lids with the beaten egg and bake in the preheated oven for 20 minutes or until brown.

Meanwhile, if making fresh anolini or tortellini, follow instructions on pages 29 and 40 and use the pork and Brussels sprouts filling on page 156. Then cook the pasta in plenty of boiling salted water for 4–5 minutes or until *al dente*. Drain and mix with the cream, nutmeg, ham and Parmesan. Season with salt and pepper to taste, and warm this filling through together. Remove the pastry from the oven and place the cases on warmed serving plates. Divide the pasta filling between the cases, and put the little lid on top. Serve hot.

Insalata di Spirali con Fagiolini e Zucchini alla Menta

{ Spiral Pasta Salad with Minted Green Beans and Courgettes }

I discovered quite recently that when I cook two of my favourite dishes – minted beans and minted courgettes – and have leftovers, they combine perfectly with pasta for a flavoursome and refreshing salad.

SERVES 4

300g dried spirali pasta
salt and pepper, to taste
1 tbsp extra virgin olive oil

SALAD
300g tender green beans, trimmed
500g courgettes, halved, then cut into quarters
2 garlic cloves, peeled and sliced
60ml extra virgin olive oil
20ml strong white wine vinegar
3 tbsp fresh mint leaves

Cook the pasta in advance so that it can cool. Cook in plenty of boiling salted water for 8–9 minutes or until *al dente*. Drain, dress with the olive oil, then leave to cool.

In another large pan, bring plenty of salted water to the boil and cook the beans first for about 10 minutes until they are softish. Scoop them out using a slotted spoon, and cook the courgettes in the same water for 8–10 minutes. Drain and combine them with the beans in a large bowl with the garlic, the olive oil, the vinegar and some salt and pepper. Mix well and leave to marinate until cold.

Add the mint and mix with the pasta. Taste again for salt and pepper and serve.

Insalata di Trofie, Fave, Cipolle e Pecorino

{ Short Pasta Salad with Broad Beans, Balsamic Onions and Pecorino }

I could have used gramigna pasta for this salad. Gramigna is a prime example of how the Italian imagination, when giving names to pasta, is bewildering, to say the least. *Gramigna* is a plant known as Bermuda grass, which spreads very readily, becoming a garden pest. It is not clear to me how a short piece of pasta bent into a semi-circle could be likened to the plant, but the pasta pieces look pretty in salads, and taste good, as do the more readily available trofie...

SERVES 4

300g dried trofie (or gramigna) pasta
salt and pepper, to taste
1 tbsp extra virgin olive oil

SALAD
1kg young broad beans, podded
60ml extra virgin olive oil
200g small onions, peeled
30g caster sugar
2 tbsp balsamic vinegar
200g pecorino cheese, cut into small strips

Cook the pasta in advance so that it can cool. Cook in plenty of boiling salted water for 12–14 minutes or until *al dente*. Drain, dress with the olive oil, then leave to cool.

Blanch the beans in a large saucepan of lightly salted water, a few minutes only. Remove from the water with a slotted spoon. When cool enough to handle, remove the outer skin, revealing the bright green beans inside. Sauté these gently in the oil for a few minutes. Lift them from the pan and set aside.

Blanch the onions in the same salted water, until soft, about 15 minutes. Scoop out and fry them for a few minutes in the same oil and the same pan as the broad beans. Add the sugar, let it caramelise a little on the heat, and then add the balsamic vinegar and a little water if needed. Let it cool. (These onions are also very good as a pickled part of an antipasto.)

Mix the balsamic onions and all their juices with the broad beans, the cheese and the pasta. Season to taste with salt and pepper, and serve.

Insalata di Gomiti con Peperoni e Capperi

{ Salad of Elbow Pasta with Peppers and Capers }

This is a very refreshing summer salad for picnics or barbecues. It came about because I had leftovers from a salad of roasted peppers. All I had to do than was to choose complementary ingredients. You'll get the best flavours from the peppers if you charcoal-grill them.

SERVES 4

300g dried gomiti pasta
salt and pepper, to taste
1 tbsp extra virgin olive oil

SALAD
400g sweet peppers, red and yellow
　(not green)
1 large garlic clove, peeled and crushed
50ml extra virgin olive oil
150g salted capers, rinsed
2 tbsp coarsely chopped fresh flat-leaf parsley

ALTERNATIVES

The elbow pasta can be substituted by penne or butterfly pasta (farfalle).

Cook the pasta in advance so that it can cool. Cook in plenty of boiling salted water for 6–7 minutes or until *al dente*. Drain, dress with the olive oil, then leave to cool.

Have your barbecue ready, and cook the peppers whole until the skin is charred and black. Or hold the peppers over a gas flame – but the flavour won't be the same. Cool, then remove the skins. Cut the peppers in half, and remove the seeds and pith. Cut the flesh into strips lengthways and mix with the garlic and the olive oil in a large salad bowl. Leave to rest and let the flavours infuse.

Add the washed capers, parsley and pasta to the peppers and mix everything together well. To finish, sprinkle with salt and pepper.

Insalata di Orzo con Sottaceti e Tonno

{ Pasta Salad with Pickles and Tuna }

A very appetising salad for the summer but many would also appreciate it as an *antipasto*. It is a very quick salad considering the ingredients are all preserved, and if you find a very good deli you can buy everything from there.

SERVES 4

200g dried orzo pasta
salt and pepper, to taste
1 tbsp extra virgin olive oil

MARINATED CUCUMBER
150g cucumber, cut into strips, cut into strips
1 tsp caster sugar
1 tbsp white wine vinegar

SALAD
200g small onions, preserved in balsamic
  vinegar, cut into little chunks
100g sun-blush tomatoes, cut into strips
20g small salted capers, rinsed
1 tbsp fresh oregano leaves
200g good canned tuna in oil, drained and
  roughly flaked
juice of ½ lemon
80ml extra virgin olive oil

ALTERNATIVES
You could use ditalini or farfalline instead of the orzo.

Cook the pasta in advance so that it can cool. Cook in plenty of boiling salted water for 5 minutes or until *al dente*. Drain, dress with the olive oil, then leave to cool.

Marinate the cucumber strips in the sugar, salt and vinegar for half an hour.

Once the pasta has cooled, mix it with the cucumber and all the prepared salad ingredients in a large salad bowl. Drizzle with the lemon juice and the olive oil. Season with lots of pepper, and taste to see if it needs any salt.

Insalata Caprese con Spaghetti Rotti

{ Broken Spaghetti Salad with Tomato and Mozzarella }

An *insalata caprese* is a classic mozzarella and tomato combination. I have given this classic a little twist by adding pasta, but the recipe still remains very Italian. For the pasta I have used broken spaghetti, as people often do in the absence of shorter pasta. The salad is extremely simple to make.

SERVES 4

250g dried spaghetti pasta
salt and pepper, to taste
1 tbsp extra virgin olive oil

SALAD

3 large very ripe and beefy tomatoes, chopped
2 large buffalo mozzarella balls (125g each),
    very fresh, sliced
80ml extra virgin olive oil
2 tbsp white wine vinegar
20 fresh basil leaves

Cook the pasta in advance so that it can cool. Break it first into pieces of 6–7cm in length. Cook in plenty of boiling salted water for 5–6 minutes or until *al dente*. Drain, dress with the olive oil, then leave to cool.

Cut the tomatoes in eighths first and then into chunks. Cut the mozzarella into thick slices first then into small cubes. In a large bowl, mix the pasta, tomatoes and mozzarella, then pour over the oil followed by the vinegar and some salt and pepper to taste. Cover with basil leaves and serve.

ALTERNATIVE

You could use vermicelli instead of spaghetti.

Insalata di Fusilli e Funghi

{ Spiral Pasta and Pickled Wild Mushroom Salad }

There is nothing quite like a pasta salad, especially in the late summer when it can be made with wild mushrooms, the picking of which is one of my greatest passions. Here is one of my favourites. (For alternatives to wild mushrooms see page 144.)

SERVES 4

300g dried fusilli pasta
salt and pepper, to taste
1 tbsp extra virgin olive oil
juice of 1 lemon
fresh sprigs of oregano or marjoram, plus
    extra for serving

MUSHROOMS
800g (cleaned weight) mixed wild mushrooms
    or cultivated chestnut mushrooms,
    chanterelles, oysters etc.
4 tbsp good white wine vinegar
5 cloves
½ tsp ground cinnamon
1 small fresh hot red chilli
2 garlic cloves, unpeeled
4 bay leaves
5 tbsp extra virgin olive oil
1 tbsp fresh oregano or marjoram
2 tbsp coarsely chopped fresh flat-leaf parsley

Cook the pasta in advance so that it can cool. Cook in plenty of boiling salted water for 8–10 minutes or until *al dente*. Drain, dress with the olive oil and lemon juice, and leave to cool.

Clean the mushrooms carefully, wiping rather than washing them.

In a large saucepan, bring 1.5 litres water to the boil. Add the vinegar, 20g salt, the cloves, cinnamon, chilli, garlic and bay leaves and cook together for a few minutes for the flavours to infuse. Add the mushrooms and cook for 10 minutes. Drain the mushrooms well, and mix with the oil and herbs. Leave to cool.

Mix the 'pickled' mushrooms with the pasta, taste for salt, add some black pepper and a sprinkle of oregano or marjoram and parsley and enjoy!

Insalata di Penne Integrali con Spugnole e Orecchie di Giuda

{ Wholemeal Pasta Salad with Morels and Judas' Ears }

'Nature with nature' is the motto of this dish. One of the many types of pasta available is wholemeal pasta, which I like to marry with wild mushrooms in a tasty salad. Morels are available dried from good delicatessens. Judas' ears can be found in the wild attached to elder trees, especially after a period of rain, but they are also sold dried in Chinese shops as 'black fungus'. Both mushrooms return to normal size when soaked in water.

SERVES 4

350g dried wholemeal penne pasta
salt and pepper, to taste
1–2 tbsp extra virgin olive oil

SALAD
40g dried morel mushrooms, rehydrated
40g dried Judas' ear mushrooms, rehydrated
70ml olive oil
2 garlic cloves, peeled and sliced
1 small fresh hot red chilli, chopped
2 tbsp chopped fresh flat-leaf parsley
juice of 1 lemon

Rehydrate the mushrooms first. Soak the morels for 1 hour in lukewarm water. Soak the Judas' ears in cold water for 30 minutes.

Meanwhile, cook the pasta in plenty of boiling salted water for 8–10 minutes or until *al dente*. Drain, dress with the olive oil, then leave to cool.

Clean the mushrooms quickly with your fingers, squeeze out any excessive water. Heat the oil in a frying pan, and fry the mushrooms, garlic and chilli briefly for 5 minutes. Add salt and pepper, the parsley and lemon juice. Leave to cool, then mix well with the pasta and serve.

Insalata di Mare Fredda con Penne senza Glutine

{ Salad of Gluten-free Pasta with Seafood }

It is very good to know that people who are allergic to gluten can now enjoy pasta. Gluten-free pastas are made from maize and rice flours, even lentils, in limited shapes as yet. I am very pleased that the Carluccio's chain is offering gluten-free pasta, and wish every establishment would be as aware.

SERVES 4

300g dried gluten-free penne pasta
salt and pepper, to taste
1 tbsp extra virgin olive oil

SALAD
800g mixed seafood, cleaned weight, such
   as small octopus, cuttlefish, mussels, squid
   (cut into rings), prawns, scallops (with
   corals), clams, etc.
1 garlic clove, peeled and crushed
3 tbsp coarsely chopped fresh flat-leaf parsley
1 bunch fresh dill, finely chopped
1 bunch fresh chives, finely chopped
70ml extra virgin olive oil
juice of 1 lemon

ALTERNATIVES

Naturally this dish can be made with ordinary pasta, The seafood can be tweaked, depending on what you can find. The herbs in this salad can also be varied depending on what you have to hand, coriander and basil would be more than acceptable.

Cook the pasta in advance so that it can cool. Cook in plenty of boiling salted water for a slightly shorter time than normal penne. However as gluten-free pasta timings can vary, best to follow the instructions on the packet or until the pasta is *al dente*. When cooked, add some fresh hot water to the pasta cooking water and then drain, dress with the olive oil and leave to cool.

Have ready another large saucepan of boiling salted water. Choose first the seafood that needs longer cooking, like the octopus and cuttlefish, and blanch them for about 12 minutes or until tender. Mussels, squid, prawns, scallops and clams will need less time, perhaps 2–4 minutes. Drain all the seafood well, and put in a large bowl. Leave to cool, then mix with the garlic, herbs, the olive oil and lastly the lemon juice. Mix in the pasta, taste for salt and pepper and serve.

Insalata di Polpo, Piselli e Pennette

{ Salad of Octopus, Peas and Pasta }

In Italian I call this the three 'P's' salad, for obvious reasons! It's a combination of mine, three delicious items beginning with the letter 'P' coming together to create something which is very appetising and at the same time very Italian.

SERVES 4

300g dried pennette (small penne) pasta
salt and pepper, to taste
1 tbsp extra virgin olive oil

SALAD
40ml olive oil
1 large onion, peeled and finely sliced
300g fresh garden peas, podded weight
1 small octopus, about 250g
finely grated zest and juice of 1 lemon
a few fresh mint leaves, chopped

Cook the pasta in advance so that it can cool. Cook in plenty of boiling salted water for 6–8 minutes or until *al dente*. Drain, dress with the olive oil, then leave to cool.

Heat the oil in a large frying pan and fry the onion for 2 minutes. Add the peas and 2 tbsp water and cook until the water has evaporated and the peas are tender. In a separate pan, cook the octopus in boiling salted water for about 18 minutes or until tender, then drain and cut into pieces. Leave everything to cool.

When everything is cool, mix together the pasta, peas, onion and oil, the octopus and lemon juice. Sprinkle with the lemon zest, mint and taste for salt and pepper.

Insalata di Couscous

{ Couscous Salad with Raw Vegetables }

This is a delightful summer salad to be eaten in summer or spring, when vegetables are at their freshest. It makes use of a larger-than-life couscous, which in Hebrew is known as '*ptitim*', and everywhere else as Israeli, pearl or giant couscous. It is made from hard wheat, and was originally shaped into pellets, though it is now available in different shapes such as hearts and stars, which are very popular with children.

SERVES 4

200g dried giant couscous
salt and pepper, to taste
1 tbsp extra virgin olive oil

SALAD
2 celery stalks
1 red pepper
1 yellow pepper
½ cucumber
4 spring onions
4 asparagus spears
½ avocado
1 apple
1 pear
good handfuls of fresh mint and parsley,
    very finely chopped
60ml extra virgin olive oil
juice of 1 lemon

Cook the couscous in advance so that it can cool. Cook in plenty of boiling salted water for 12–14 minutes or until *al dente* (follow the instructions on the packet). Dress with the olive oil, then leave to cool.

Now you need some patience. After cleaning your vegetables and fruit, cut them all into cubes, just slightly larger than the couscous. Mix them and the herbs into the cooled pasta. Add the olive oil, lemon juice, salt and abundant pepper, mix well and enjoy.

ALTERNATIVES

Ready-made fregola could be substituted for the couscous and the salad, with its mixture of vegetables, it makes a delicious filling for Greek vine leaves.

Pasta Fritta
{ Fried Pasta }

SERVES 4

200g fresh egg pasta dough (see page 29)
salt and generous black pepper, to taste
some chilli powder (optional)
olive oil, for deep-frying
Parma ham or cheese, to serve (optional)

Make the fresh egg pasta dough as usual, but adding salt and lots of pepper, and some chilli powder if wanted. Roll it out to 2mm thick, and cut into long strips of about 4cm wide.

Deep-fry these strips in hot olive oil until crisp. Drain well on absorbent kitchen paper, and serve immediately as an accompaniment to Parma ham or cheese, or just by itself.

ALTERNATIVES

To vary this popular pasta snack, which is good for using up any fresh egg pasta you may have leftover from making a recipe, try using celery salt instead of ordinary salt. You you could even experiment with other spices, replacing the chilli powder with cumin, or perhaps some dried herbs (but not basil, as this does not dry successfully). For a different flavour you could replace the olive oil used for frying with lard instead.

Frittata del Presidente
{ Leftover Pasta Omelette }

SERVES 4

30ml extra virgin olive oil
400g leftover pasta, already cooked and dressed
6 medium eggs, beaten
60g Parmesan, freshly grated
salt and pepper, to taste

Heat the olive oil in a frying pan, then add the pasta. Stir-fry for a few minutes to heat the pasta through. Mix the beaten eggs and the Parmesan, season with some salt and pepper and pour all the eggs on to the pasta. Fry gently until the base of the omelette solidifies, moving the egg from the sides to the middle. When you see that the top is also starting to solidify, then you invert the omelette, either with the help of a large plate or the large flat lid of a saucepan. When turned over, slide the softer, top side of the omelette into the pan. Fry for a little longer to set and cook this side. (You might need to add a little more oil.)

Serve in slices, hot or cold. If you want to take it to the office for lunch, or on picnics, you can make it in smaller pans, for what I would call a 'pasta burger'!

ALTERNATIVES

The best pasta to use for this substantial pasta snack, which I have dedicated to the Italian President Giorgio Napolitano, as it is his favourite comfort food, is one that has been flavoured with a tomato- or meat-based sauce, less so fish. You could add a couple of tbsp of chopped fresh flat-leaf parsley to the eggs before cooking. You could add other leftovers: if you have any roasted peppers going spare, they are wonderful in a frittata.

PASTA COME DOLCE

PASTA AS DESSERT

The idea of pasta as pudding might sound strange, though if you remember that the British can make simple bread and butter taste delicious as a pudding, then the idea isn't quite so surprising. For pasta, just like bread, is made of flour and water. It's what you add to it that makes it interesting. I am sure this is how the concept came to light anyway: in the few regions that have pasta desserts, they would have been developed by the poor people who didn't have many sophisticated ingredients to cook with; perhaps some sugar, a little dried fruit. But add syrups, foreign spices and a multitude of fruits – the prerogative of the wealthier *signori* – and the plain becomes beautiful!

Many of these pasta dishes are my own, a few are classic or regional. Some of them are fond memories of when I lived abroad, the dumplings for instance: Austrian-inspired desserts that have often been incorporated into the northern Italian repertoire. I have also included some other desserts that are made of flour and water, but may not be strictly considered to be pasta: pastry, for instance, is basically the same as pasta, with the addition of fat, which allows the dough to be baked rather than boiled in water. Pastry is a close cousin of pasta, as are pancakes, so here I have taken a bit of poetic pasta licence... The most important thing is that everything will taste delicious anyway.

And of course, die-hard pasta aficionados like eating pasta in any shape or form...

Gnocchi con Prugne

{ Prune Dumplings }

While touring the world, those interested in food always collect food experiences, and I am no different. This typical Austrian recipe from Vienna, where I spent a few years, is a sweetened gnocchi-type dumpling – known in German as *Knödel* – which is usually made with ripe apricots. The recipe I give you here is made with prunes which, because they are not seasonal like apricots, give you the freedom to cook the dish at any time of year.

SERVES 4

200g floury potatoes, peeled
600g Italian '00' flour
1 medium egg, beaten
40g caster sugar
12 pitted large semi-dried prunes, soaked in
    orange juice to cover for 15 minutes
12 sugar cubes

TO SERVE
60g unsalted butter
50g fresh breadcrumbs
½ tsp ground cinnamon
icing sugar

ALTERNATIVES

I could recommend that you try the original, with fresh apricots, but these must be very ripe. You could try it with a large, ripe strawberry or with halved Victoria plums. You could try it with semi-dried apricots as well. Like the prunes, these should be soaked in orange juice first. None of these alternatives would need the sugar lump.

Boil the floury potatoes until tender, then reduce to a purée or mash well. Mix in the flour, egg and sugar, and knead lightly to obtain a soft dough. Drain the prunes from the orange juice.

Take a piece of dough the size of the prune and flatten in the palm of your hand to make a round, quite thin container. Position one drained prune in the centre with a sugar cube inside. Close the dumpling, folding it around, or use a little extra dough to help close it, if needed. Seal in the shape of a ball. Do the same with the remaining dough, prunes and sugar cubes. You should have 12 dumplings.

Cook the dumplings in plenty of boiling water for 10 minutes or until you see them floating to the surface, which means they are ready.

Meanwhile, heat the butter in a medium saucepan and add the breadcrumbs and cinnamon. Take the dumplings out of the water using a slotted spoon, drain well and divide between warmed dessert plates. Sprinkle them with the spiced buttery breadcrumbs and some icing sugar, and serve hot.

Fettuccine di Cioccolato

{ Chocolate Noodles }

This is one for the die-hard pasta lover! You can make chocolate pasta from scratch – and I tell you how to do it on page 31 – but fortunately for those short of time it can also be bought dried from good delicatessens. This manufactured pasta is usually combined with game dishes and game sauces, but works very well with a sweet sauce here too.

SERVES 4

250g fresh chocolate pasta (see page 31)
    or 200g dried cocoa fettuccine
salt
icing sugar, for sprinkling

SAUCE
50g unsalted butter
10g cardamom pods, use only the little seeds
30g pine kernels, toasted
30g shelled hazelnuts, toasted and crushed
40g caster sugar
40g dried breadcrumbs
1 tbsp Strega or other Italian liqueur

Roll out the pasta dough, by hand or machine, to a longish sheet of about 3mm thick. Roll and cut into strips as described on page 33.

For the sauce, melt the butter in a large pan. Add the cardamom seeds, pine kernels and hazelnuts and fry a little. Add the sugar and the breadcrumbs and fry gently until they brown. Add the liqueur.

Meanwhile, cook the pasta in plenty of boiling salted water for 4–5 minutes (6–7 minutes for dried) or until *al dente*. Drain well. Dress and flavour the pasta with the sweet mixture and sprinkle with icing sugar.

SERVING SUGGESTION

A glass of Moscato sweet wine would accompany the dish well.

Budino di Fregola e Fragole

{ Strawberry Pasta Cooked in Milk, with Strawberry Sauce }

Fregola is a lovely Sardinian pasta in the shape of a pellet. It can be cooked rather like rice, and this, I suppose, is a sort of Italian pasta (rice) pudding. It is cooked with milk, flavoured with honey (orange-blossom or chestnut blossom are the most delicious) and served with a strawberry sauce.

SERVES 4

200g dried fregola pasta
salt
1 litre full-fat milk
3 tbsp clear orange-blossom honey

SAUCE
300g ripe strawberries
60g caster sugar
juice of ½ lemon

ALTERNATIVES

Try substituting the strawberries with raspberries, or even blackberries later in the year, for a different but still delicious flavour. And in place of the fregola you could use orzo instead, a pasta which already looks like rice!

Cook the pasta in plenty of boiling, slightly salted water for 10 minutes, then drain and keep aside. Add the milk to the saucepan, bring to the boil, then add the pasta and a pinch of salt. Cook the pasta until very soft and creamy, about 30 minutes. Stir in the honey and set aside to cool.

Cut the strawberries and put them in a small saucepan with the sugar and lemon juice. Over a gentle heat, let it all dissolve together to a thick sauce, helping the strawberries along occasionally with a fork. Let the sauce cool.

Eat the pasta and sauce together.

Crespelle Ripiene con Salsa di Cioccolato

{ Ricotta-stuffed Pancakes with Chocolate Sauce }

This is another recipe that reminds me of my time spent in Vienna. What they call *Palatschinken* there, actually originates from Hungary, but apart from the name the dish could well be Italian. The Viennese use a cheese called *Topfen*, which is a slightly sour curd cheese like quark. The use of cow's milk ricotta here makes this version both very Italian, and very good!

SERVES 4

PASTA COMO DOLCE

PANCAKES
140g Italian '00' flour
a pinch of salt
2 medium eggs, beaten
250ml milk
clarified butter, for frying

SAUCE
150g bitter chocolate, broken into pieces
150ml double cream
4 tbsp water
50g caster sugar

FILLING
500g fresh ricotta cheese
50g caster sugar
finely grated rind of ½ lemon

To make the pancakes, sift the flour into a bowl with the salt, and make a well in the middle. Put the eggs in the middle along with a little of the milk, and start to mix together, using a whisk. Gradually whisk in the remaining milk, and whisk until the batter is smooth.

Heat some clarified butter in a 15cm, preferably non-stick, pancake pan, just enough to moisten the base. Pour in just enough batter to cover the base, and cook gently until the bottom of the pancake is brown. Flip it over and cook the other side. All this will take a couple of minutes only. Continue with more butter and batter until you have eight thin pancakes. Set aside, wrapped in a clean tea towel to keep warm.

Meanwhile, put the chocolate sauce ingredients into the top of a double boiler (or a heatproof bowl set over a pan of simmering water), and melt together, stirring once or twice. Set aside, but keep warm.

Working quickly, mix the ricotta with the sugar and lemon rind. Put 2 tbsp of this into the middle of each pancake, and roll to obtain a sort of cannelloni. Divide between warmed plates, two each, and pour the liquid chocolate sauce on top.

Sebadas/Gnocco Sardo Fritto

{ Sardinian Fried Dumplings }

This Sardinian speciality, which is both sweet and savoury at the same time, makes good use of fresh pecorino cheese (also known as *caciotta*, and one of the best Sardinian ingredients) as well as the superb local orange-blossom honey.

SERVES 4 (MAKES 4 LARGE RAVIOLI)

200g fresh egg pasta dough (see page 29)
50g caster sugar
2 tsp Marsala red wine
100g fresh and soft pecorino cheese,
    cut into 4 squares, about 8cm diameter
olive oil, for deep- or shallow-frying

TO SERVE
100g clear orange-blossom honey

Make the pasta as described on page 30, adding the sugar and Marsala, which will produce a softer dough. Wrap in cling film and let it rest in the fridge for 20 minutes.

Roll out the dough either by machine or with a rolling pin to a thickness of 2mm. Cut out eight large circles of 15cm in diameter. Cover with a damp tea towel while you prepare everything else.

Place one piece of cheese in the middle of one pasta circle, and wet the edges. Cover with another pasta circle, and press with a fork around the borders to seal the parcel. Do the same with the remaining pasta and cheese.

Fry the dumplings in hot oil until golden on both sides: you will need to turn them if shallow-frying. Serve hot with some orange-blossom honey poured on top.

Torta di Pasta Tipo Pastiera
{ Neapolitan Ricotta Pasta Tart }

The *pastiera* is one of the best-known tarts in the south of Italy, especially in Campania, where Neapolitan artisan bakers produce this speciality in great quantities. It has an Easter connection because using cooked wheat grains has a religious significance. Here I have substituted the usual grain with small pasta and the result is surprisingly good.

SERVES 6 OR MORE

PASTRY
250g plain flour
125g lard, cut into small chunks
a pinch of salt
25g caster sugar
1 medium egg, beaten
unsalted butter, for greasing

FILLING
250g dried fregola pasta
salt
3 medium eggs
125g caster sugar
3 tbsp orange-blossom water
¾ tsp ground cinnamon
350g fresh ricotta cheese, sheep's milk, preferably
75g candied citron peel, roughly chopped
75g candied orange peel, roughly chopped
icing sugar, for dusting

For the pastry, sift the flour on to your work surface, and work in the lard until the texture is like crumbs. Mix in the salt and sugar. Make a well in the centre, and pour in the beaten egg. Gradually work the flour into the egg until you have a smooth pastry. Wrap in cling film and chill in the fridge for an hour.

Preheat the oven to 180°C/Gas 4.

Cook the pasta in plenty of lightly salted boiling water for 9 minutes (instead of 12) or until still *al dente*. Drain and set aside.

Separate the eggs and whisk the whites to a stiff white snow in a large bowl. Beat the egg yolks with the sugar, then add the orange-blossom water, cinnamon, ricotta, citron and orange peel. Mix thoroughly, then mix in the pasta. Fold in the beaten egg white.

Lightly grease a baking tin of 18cm diameter, 7–8cm high. Roll out the pastry to 1mm thick, then use this to line the bottom and sides of the tin. Leave some pastry to cut into long strips for a lattice on top of the filling, if liked.

Pour the pasta and ricotta mixture into the tin, cutting the excess pastry from around the rim. Cover with lattice strips if you like. Bake the tart in the preheated oven for 45–50 minutes until set and golden. Leave it to cool and set. Sprinkle with icing sugar and serve in small wedges. *Buona Pasqua.*

Ravioloni Dolci con Marmellata

{ Baked Pastry Squares Stuffed with Jam }

In our household, when I was a child, this was the best way of using up some of the huge amounts of jam my mother used to make during the season. It was always a delight to come home from school and find these stuffed baked parcels for tea. With six of us to cater for, huge quantities were made each time. The addition of butter to this basic pasta dough (flour and eggs) makes the dough shorter, which makes it more like a pastry and enables it to be baked.

MAKES 24 PARCELS

PASTRY
300g Italian '00' flour
a pinch of salt
3 medium eggs, beaten
75g unsalted butter, melted and cooled, plus extra for greasing

TO FINISH
400g jam of your choice
icing sugar, for sprinkling

To make the pastry, sift the flour into a bowl with the salt, and make a well in the middle. Put the eggs in the middle along with the melted butter, and start to mix the flour from the sides into the liquid ingredients. Mix with your fingers until everything is amalgamated, and you have a smooth pastry. Wrap in cling film, and let the dough rest for an hour in the fridge.

Preheat the oven to 180°C/Gas 4.

With a rolling pin or a pasta machine roll the dough out to sheets 3mm thick and as long as you can. Cut into bands 12cm wide and position a tsp of jam at 5cm intervals (each tsp placed closer to one edge of band than the other). Brush some water around the jam. Cover the dollops of jam by folding the other long side of the pasta over the filling and press with your hands all round the jam dollops to seal the ravioloni. Cut with a pastry cutter and put the parcels on a greased baking tray.

Bake in the preheated oven for 15–20 minutes. Serve hot, sprinkled with icing sugar, or leave to cool. Either is delicious.

A LIST OF PASTAS

Even for an Italian it is very difficult to find a way through the jungle of pasta names, for there are more than 600 different shapes and names, not necessarily counting those that are added from the private point of view, of restaurants, for instance. And of course, the habits and traditions of different regions complicates things further: a pasta in one region may have the same name as a pasta in another region – but they might be completely different in shape!

ACINI DI PEPE | Peppercorn-sized pasta, small for *brodo*

AGNOLINI/ANOLINI | Fresh stuffed, round or half-moon wrapped (belly-button), from Parma/Mantua. Smaller than tortellini

AGNOLOTTI | Square-shaped stuffed egg pasta

AGNOLOTTI DEL PLIN | Rectangular little bags with pinched ends

ALFABETO/LETTERE | Alphabet pasta shapes, small for *brodo*

ANELLI/ANELLINI/ANNELLETTI | Thin rings of dried pasta, small for *brodo* and *timbales*, from Sicily

ANGIULOTTUS | Like the Piedmontese agnolotti or ravioli, but from Sardinia

ANOLINI/AGNOLINI | Fresh stuffed, round or half-moon wrapped (belly-button), from Parma/Mantua. Smaller than tortellini

BAVETTE/BAVETTINE/LINGUE DI PASSERO | Long narrow ribbon pasta, flattened rather than round, narrower than tagliatelle

BIGOLI | Long and thick spaghetti, often made with buckwheat or wholewheat flour

BRANDELLI | Roughly cut or torn pieces of fresh pasta, my invention. Brandelli means 'in tatters'

BUCATINI | Thick spaghetti with a hole through the middle. Also known as perciatelli

CANDELE | Long hollow tubes, 10–15cm, the length of 'candles'

CANNARONI | Very similar to rigatoni. Zitoni pasta is often called cannaroni

CANNELLONI | Cylindrical tubes of fresh or dried egg pasta, stuffed and baked. A dish of cannelloni can also be made with *crespelle* (crepes)

CANNOLICCHI | Short tubes which are spirally grooved, rather like a screw

CAPELLI D'ANGELO/CAPELLINI | 'Angel's hair', long, very thin spaghetti

CAPPELLACCI (VERDE ETC) | Large half-moon wrapped shape, like larger tortellini

CAPPELLETTI/CAPPELLETTINI | Smaller versions of cappellacci, similar to tortellini. They may have larger wings on the side

CÂSONSÉI/CASONCELLI | Savoury stuffed fresh pasta, bent rectangular shape, from Lombardy

CASONZIEI | Stuffed fresh pasta, crescent shape, from Veneto

CAVATIELLI/CAVATOEDDO/CAVATODDO | Short solid lengths, like a doubled or tripled orecchiette, with finger indentations

CECATELLI | 2cm solid lengths indented with one finger, like an unrounded orecchiette

CHIOCCIOLE/LUMACHE/LUMACHELLE | Ridged 'snails', from Campania

CHITARRA/MANFRICOLI/TONNARELLI | Long thick square-shaped spaghetti cut on a wooden frame with wires – literally 'guitar'

CIRIOLE | A thicker version of spaghetti alla chitarra, from Umbria

CONCHIGLIE/CONCHIGLIONI/CONCHIGLIETTE | Shell shapes in varying sizes

CORZETTI/CROXETTI | Egg pasta from Liguria, pressed into coin shapes and dried

COUSCOUS | Grain-like wheat pasta, most common in Sicily. There is a giant version, known as Israeli or giant couscous. In Sardinia, knows as fregola

CULURGIONES/CULURZONES | Sardinian ravioli, often half-moon or ship's sail shaped, sometimes square or rectangular, with ruffled edges

DITALI/DITALINI/DITALONI | Short tubes of varying thickness, small for *brodo*

FAGOTTINI | Stuffed pasta, in a bundle shape, similar to plin

FARFALLE/FARFALLINE/FARFALLETTE/FARFALLONI |
Bow-tie or butterfly shapes, in varying sizes

FAZZOLETTI | Handkerchief shapes of pasta

FESTONE | Long ruffled and twisted ribbons

FETTUCCE/FETTUCCINE/FETTUCELLE | Long,
ribbon-shaped egg pasta, of varying widths. They
are generally wider than tagliatelle, and are popular
in Rome

FIDELINI/FEDELINI | Long pasta, between spaghetti
and vermicelli

FREGOLA | Bead-like pasta from Sardinia

FUSILLI | Short coiled or spiral pasta, hand- or
machine-made

FUSILLI LUNGHI (BUCATI) | Very long coiled rods

GARGANELLI | Smallish egg pasta squares rolled into
quills, hand- and machine-made

GIGANTONI/MANICHE | Large straight hollow pasta
shapes, about 6cm in length and 1.5cm in diameter

GNOCCHI | Small dumplings, made with egg, water
and flour, or with boiled potatoes and flour

GNOCCHI ALLA ROMANA | Cooked and set
semolina cut in rounds and baked with butter
and cheese

GNOCCHETTI SARDI | Small curled shell-like ovals,
ridged on one side. Can be dried or fresh. Also known
as malloreddus ('fat little calves'/'little bulls')

GRAMIGNA | A short pasta, shaped like a semi-circle
with one end turned in

GOMITI | Short bent tubes or elbows

LAIANELLE | Half-moon *ravioli*, usually filled with
ricotta, and served with a lamb or goat *ragù* (from
Abruzzo and Molise)

LASAGNE/LAGANE/LAGANELLE | Fresh pasta cut
into wide strips, also dried (festonate, with curly
edges). This was the *laganon* of the Greeks, the
laganum of the Romans

LASAGNETTE | Narrower version of lasagne,
sometimes known as riccia pasta, lasagne riccia, or
mafaldine. Has ruffled sides

LINGUINE/LINGUINETTE/LINGUETTINE | Long
flattened, spaghetti-like dried pasta, 'little tongues'.
Particularly suited to fish pasta sauces

LORIGHITTAS | Sardinian homemade pasta, spiral
rings bent into ovals

LUMACHE/LUMACHELLE | Snail shell shape

LUMACONI/PIPE | Large snail shell shape

MACCARUNI DI CASA | Homemade macaroni, also
known as scivateddi inferrittati, found in Calabria

MACCHERONI/MACCHERONCELLI/
MACCHERONCINI | Dried, short, smooth or ribbed
tubular pasta, sometimes curled

MACCHERONI ALLA CHITARRA (ALSO
MANFRICOLI/TONNARELLI) | Long thick square-
shaped spaghetti cut on a wooden frame with wires
– literally 'guitar'

MAFALDE | Rectangular ribbons, with one or both
sides ruffled

MAFALDINE | Narrower version of lasagne,
sometimes known as lasagnette, riccia pasta or
lasagne riccia. Has ruffled sides

MALLOREDDUS | Small curled shell-like ovals,
ridged on one side. Can be dried or fresh, 'fat little
calves'/'little bulls'. Also known as gnocchetti sardi

MALTAGLIATI | Rough or 'badly cut' pieces of leftover
fresh pasta, also dried

MANICHE/GIGANTONI | Large straight hollow pasta
shapes, about 6cm in length and 1.5cm in diameter

MANICOTTI | Large ridged tubes for stuffing

MANILLI DE SEA | Thin sheets of fresh pasta of
varying sizes, usually 12cm squares. 'Handkerchief of
silk' in Arabic

MUNEZZAGLIA | Mixed pasta for *pasta e fagioli*
(Naples)

ORECCHIETTE (BARESI ETC) | A small curved ear
or bowl shape, usually made with durum semolina
wheat flour, from Puglia, hand or machine-made

ORECCHIONI ROSSI/VERDI | Curved discs, ear-
shaped, red or green, fresh or dried, larger than
orecchiette

ORZO/RISI | Rice-shaped pasta, small for *brodo*

PACCHERI | Large tubes

PAGLIA E FIENO | 'Hay and straw', very thin
tagliolini, some green, some yellow

PANSÔTI | Ligurian triangular ravioli, stuffed with
greens, usually served with walnut sauce

PAPPARDELLE | Long wide ribbons of egg pasta,
fresh or dried, from 2cm wide. From Tuscany

PASSATELLI | Like Spätzle, an egg pasta or bread
mixture is pressed through holes into boiling broth.
From Emilia-Romagna

PENNE/PENNETTE/PENNONI (LISCE, SMOOTH/ RIGATE, RIDGED ETC) | Medium length tubes, cut diagonally at both ends. 'Quills' of varying sizes

PERCIATELLI/PERCIATELLINI | Long thicker bucatini

PICCAGGE | Ligurian word for fettuccine

PICI/PINCI | Very thick, long, hand-rolled strands. Pinci come from Tuscany, reminiscent of the Venetian bigoli

PIZZOCCHERI | Buckwheat tagliatelle, from Valtellina in Lombardy

QUADRUCCI | Fresh or dried pasta, usually with eggs, cut into little squares and added to soup

RAVIOLI/RAVIOLINI/RAVIOLONI | Squares of fresh egg pasta, stuffed, of varying sizes

RIGATONI | Medium-sized dried ribbed macaroni

RISTORANTI | Spaghetti in Naples

ROTOLO | Hand-rolled pasta with filling

SAGNE | Long twisted ribbons from Puglia

SCIALATELLI OR SCILATIELLI | Fresh long square-shaped spaghetti

SEADAS/SEBADAS | Large Sardinian ravioli (sweet)

SEDANI/SEDANINI | Short and thin ridged macaroni. Named because it looks like a celery stalk, ribbed outside and hollow inside

SEMI DI MELONE/SEMONI | Melon-seed shapes, small for *brodo*

SPAGHETTI/SPAGHETTINI/SPAGHETTONI | Long rounded strands of fresh or dried pasta, of varying thicknesses

SPAGHETTI ALLA CHITARRA | Long egg pasta strands, square rather than round, made on a frame of wires

SPÄTZLE | Small dumplings made by grating egg pasta dough directly into boiling water or broth. Means 'little sparrow' in Swabian German

SPIRALI | Short spirals

STELLE/STELLINE/STELLETTE/STELLETTINE | Star shapes, small for *brodo*

STRACCI | Roughly torn handkerchief shapes, similar to fazzoletti

STRANGOLAPRETE/STRANGULAPRIEVETE/ STROZZAPRETE | Literally 'priest-chokers', and even priests would lose patience with the number of different types of pasta claiming the name. Can be

very long spaghetti in coils; short lengths of fresh pasta dough rolled between the fingers, straight or twisted; and it could be made with bread, potato or actual bread dough. It is sometimes like gnocchi…

STRASCINATI (STRASCINARI) | Wheat flour pasta dough enriched with *sugna* (lard), rolled to a thin sausage over an implement called a *cavarola*, and cut into lengths to a rough macaroni shape. From Basilicata

STRINGOZZI, STRENGOZZI OR STRANGOZZI | Long, shoelace-like strands of rolled pasta, from Umbria

TAGLIATELLE/TAGLIOLINI/TAGLIERINI/ TAGLIATELLINE | Long ribbon pasta, usually 5mm wide, generally narrower than fettuccine

TAJARIN | The Piedmontese version of tagliolini. Fresh thin ribbons of pasta, usually served with a chicken liver sauce and truffles

TONNARELLI | Similar to chitarra, long pasta like tagliatelle, but with a square profile. Can be found plain white or black (with ink)

TORTELLI | Medium square or rectangular ravioli, stuffed, savoury or sweet

TORTELLINI/TORTELLONI | Stuffed fresh pasta, half-moon and wrapped (belly-button), various sizes

TORTIGLIONE | Narrower rigatoni, more deeply grooved, can be twisted

TRENETTE | Long flattened dried pasta, similar to linguine. The Genoese version of linguine

TRIA | A Puglian version of tagliatelle, used in *ciceri e tria*

TRIPOLINE | A long, large tagliatelle with a curled ribbon shape on the side

TROFIE | Little twisted pieces of pasta, dried or fresh, from Liguria

TUBETTI/TUBETTINI (LISCI ETC) | Short tubes of pasta, of varying sizes

VERMICELLI/VERMICELLINI/VERMICELLONI | Long dry rounded pasta of varying thickness. The thinnest of the long pastas. 'Little worms' as they are known in Naples

ZITI/ZITONI | Long cylindrical dried tubes of varying sizes

INDEX

B (top)